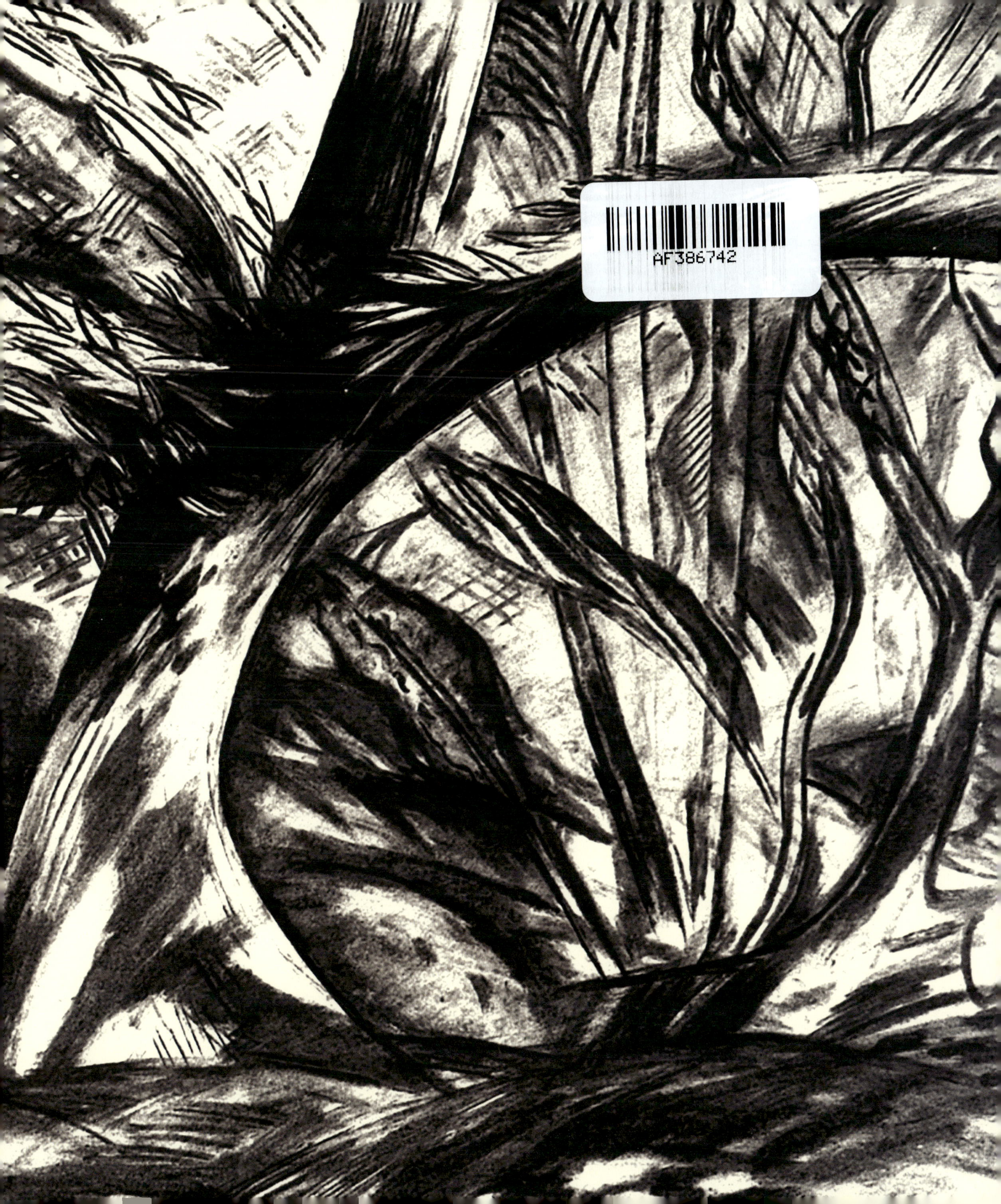
AF386742

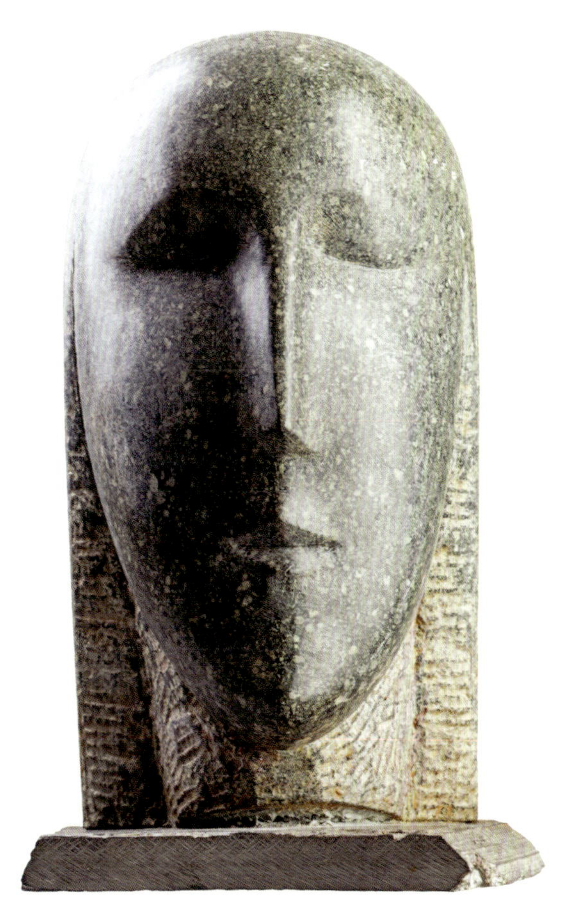

Shared Visions
Shared Lives

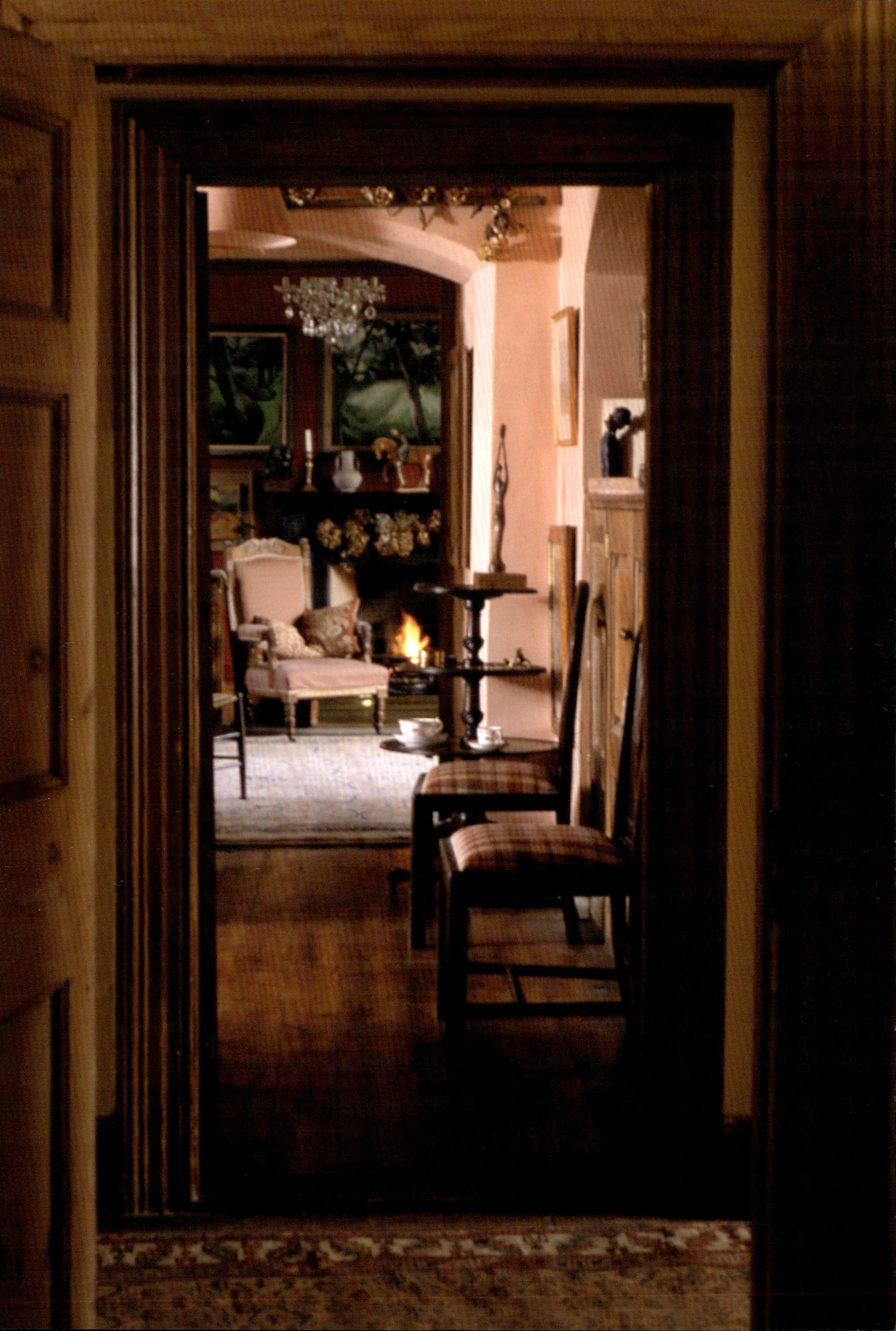

Shared Visions
Shared Lives

Briony & Andrew Lawson

IMPRESS

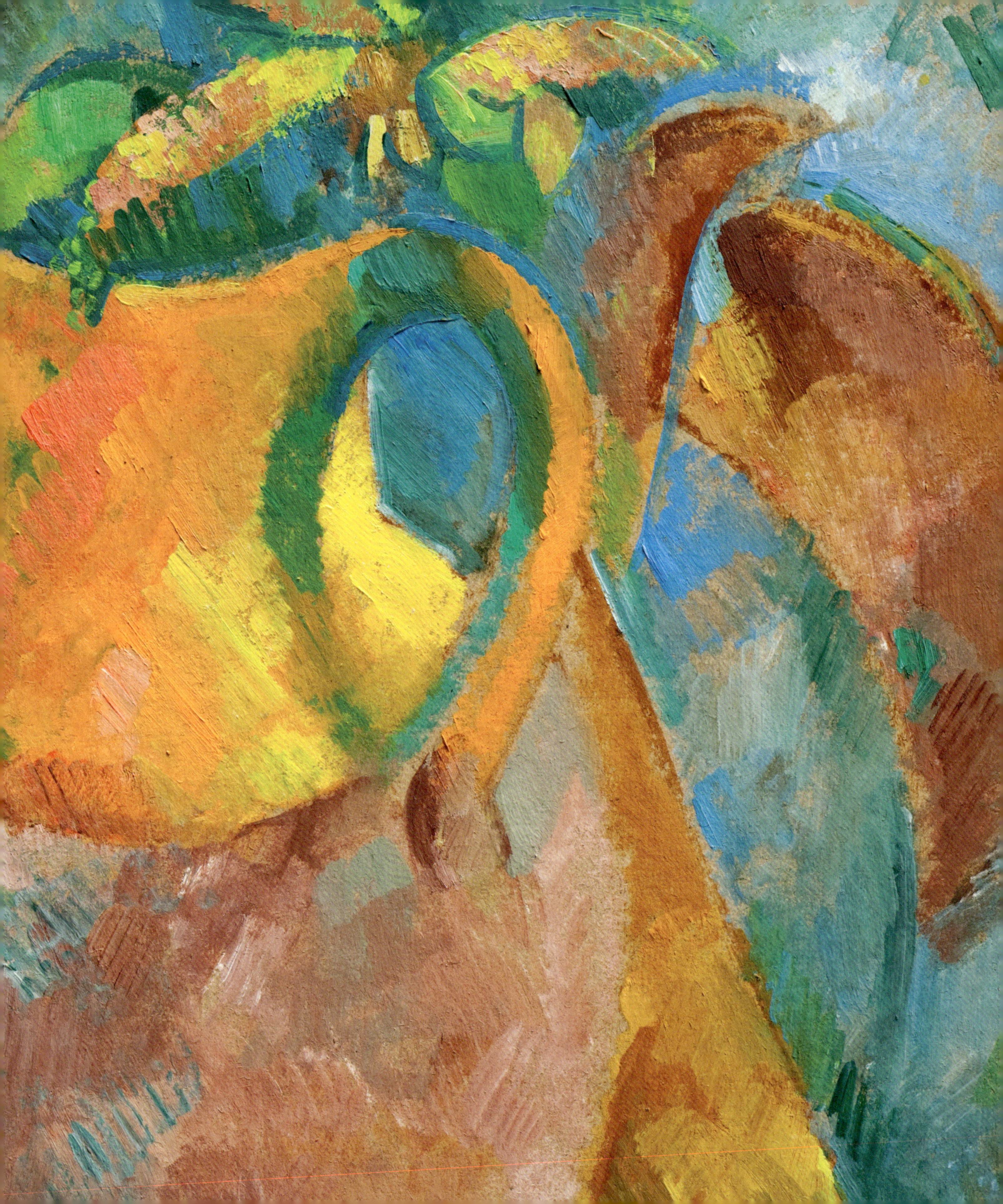

Introduction

Marking a celebratory exhibition at Gothic House, their family home in Charlbury, this book brings together highlights of sculptures and paintings by Briony and Andrew Lawson. Over the last half-century, these two artists have been inspired by their surroundings to produce a dynamic and varied body of work. Their shared passion for the North Devon landscape is infused throughout much of their work.

Briony has been sculpting in wood, stone and clay since her days as a student at City & Guilds Art School in London. Her prolific body of work draws on natural and organic subjects, often pared down to the most simple and elemental forms.

Known worldwide as a garden photographer, Andrew Lawson was trained as a painter. His painting has always informed the eye behind the camera. This book surveys Andrew's work from his early school posters and from his student days at Oxford, to his subsequent paintings that draw inspiration from his favoured woodland and sea landscapes of Devon.

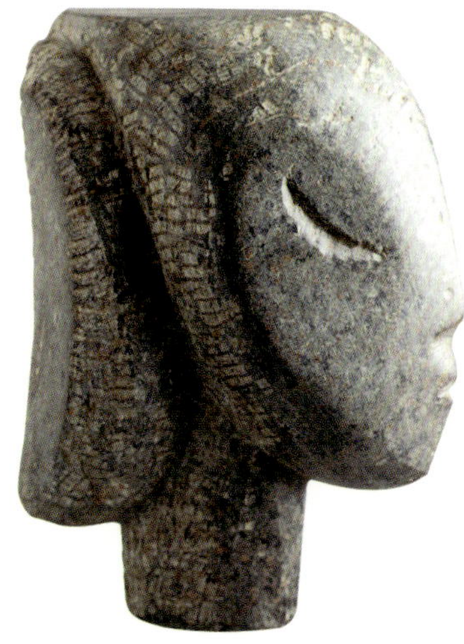

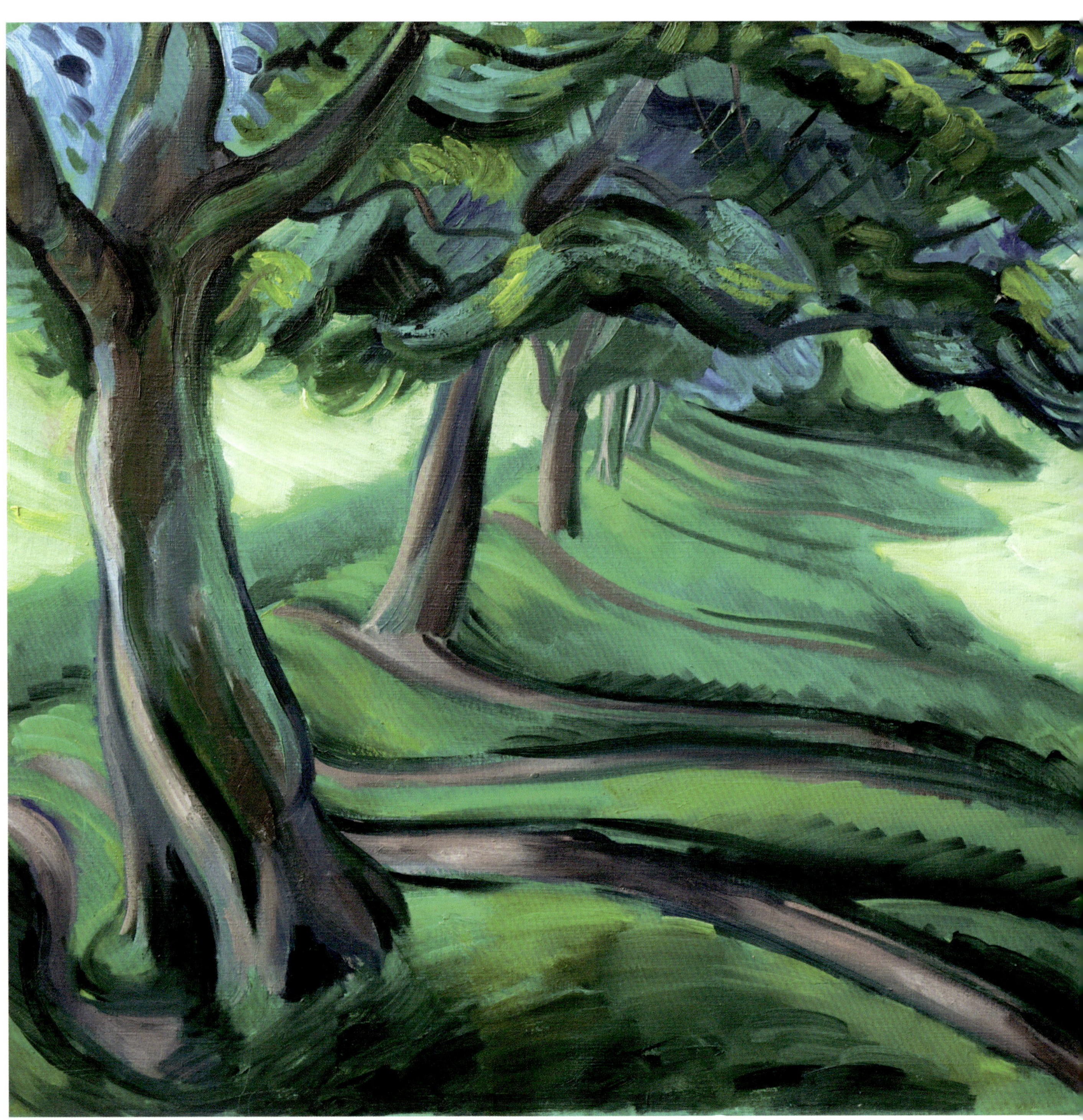

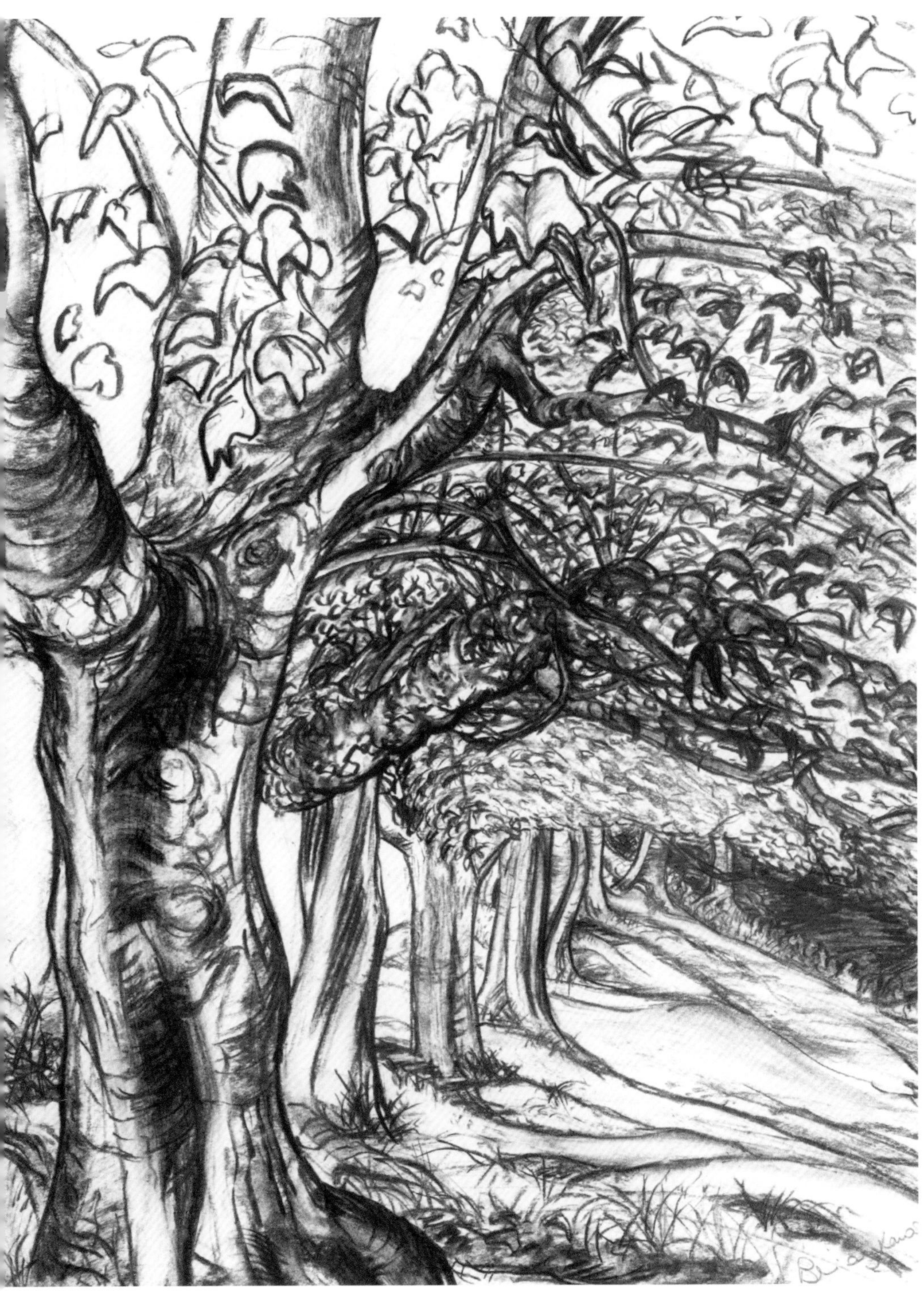

Shared Visions
It is unusual for Briony and Andrew to tackle precisely the same subject, as here. This is an avenue of sycamore trees, growing beside an ancient Devon bank. The trees are on the slope below May Brock's Cottage, in Welcombe, where Briony and Andrew lived in the early years of their marriage. The gently rolling valleys, geometric rock forms and damp, lush woodlands of Welcombe and Marsland, are the background of Briony and Andrew's shared vision.

Far Left: Andrew Lawson, *The Sycamore Bank*, 1979. Oil on Canvas

Left: Briony Lawson, *The Sycamore Bank*, 1979. Charcoal

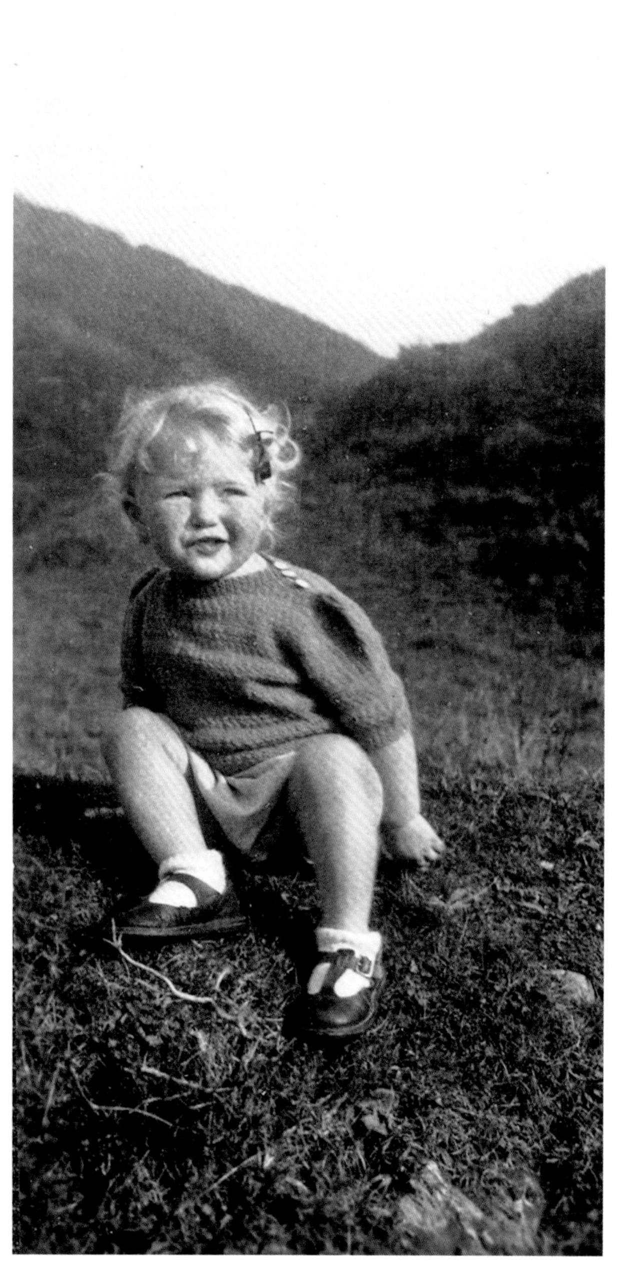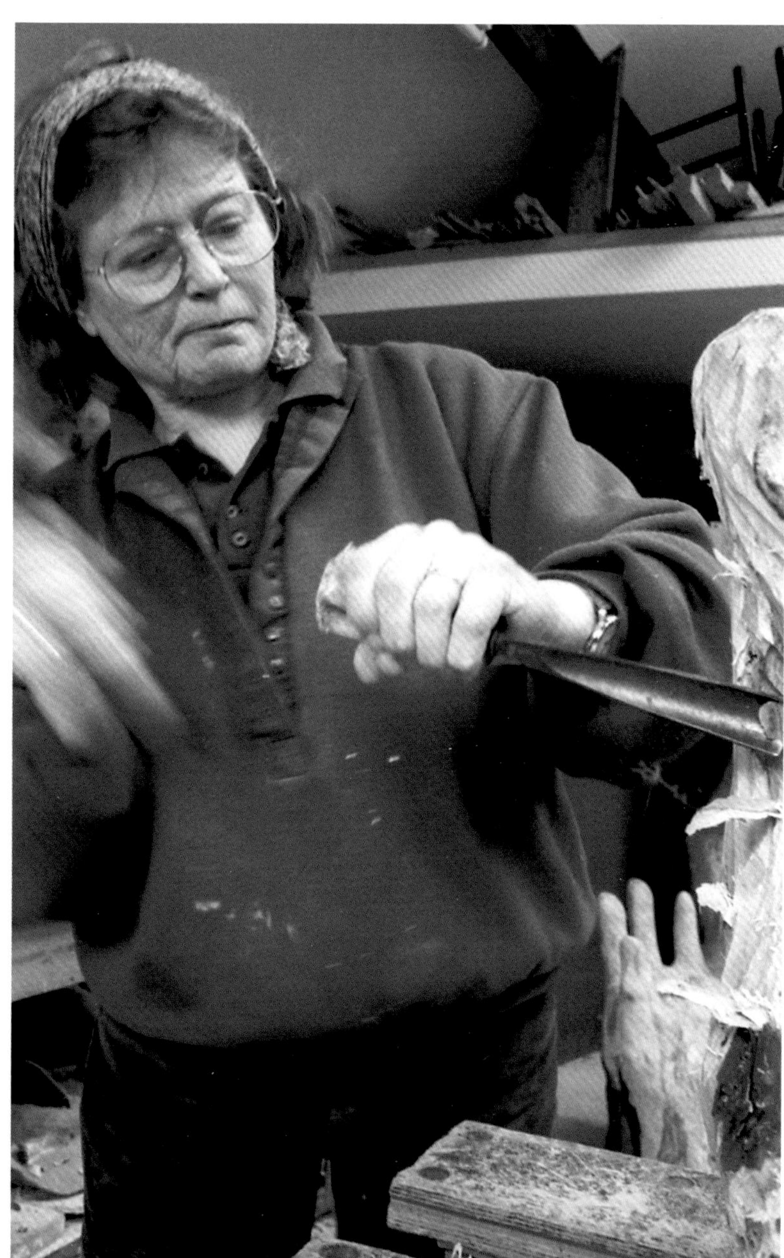

Briony Lawson

by Peter Stiles

My first contact with the sculpture of Briony Lawson came when I was quite young. At some point during the 1970s my parents and their friends booked a cottage in Welcombe, a small coastal village on the border between North Devon and Cornwall. Walking along the path that leads down into Marsland valley, Dad and his mates spotted what appeared to be a naked woman sunbathing on the terrace of a house near the beach. They used their binoculars to examine her with an intensity they concealed as if trying to distinguish a kestrel from a peregrine falcon. Someone swore that he had seen the woman move but Dad wasn't so sure. At the end of the day, when we trudged back from the beach, the young woman was still there and all the men, rather sadly, agreed that it was just a statue. If nothing else, it demonstrated that her work already had a life and energy of its own.

Much of Briony's life has been bound up with that small village where we took our holidays. The light there is softened by the Atlantic spray and at first sight the hills and valleys appear to echo the gentle rolling ocean (although it doesn't take too long to realise that neither sea nor land are quite as benign as they seem). The beauty of the place is undeniable. The location of her house is reminiscent of a Samuel Palmer landscape; the same fertile swelling forms – and Palmer would have worshipped the immense bright clouds which so often drift across the blue chalice of sky at the end of the valley.

A lot has been written about the influence of landscape on British sculpture – particularly in relation to those modernist 20th century sculptors whose work has informed Briony Lawson's art. Henry Moore talked about the way in which his sculpture took on the features of the Yorkshire countryside where he grew up and Briony admires both his work and his writing.

As I move among Briony's sculptures, between shapes that at first glance seem abstract, I begin to recognise unwinding ferns and their rippling fronds, the haunches of the cattle in the bottom of the valley and the skulls of the sheep that dot the hillside. I can see the great round boulders that the sea rolls around the beach and the strong silhouettes of the two headlands that bookend the bay. The complexities of the valley's geology – where the stream has carved intricate dips and ledges into the hillside – provide a store of forms that Briony has looked at all her life and the result of that study is clearly visible in the rhythms and balance of her sculpture.

Yet for Briony the landscape of North Devon provides much more than an encyclopaedia of abstract shapes. Her lifetime's connection with the place has made it a storehouse of memory and emotion. The parish of Welcombe is full of people and stories which continue to be woven into the fabric of her life and her work. Family legend has it that as a new-born baby, Briony was carried back from maternity hospital on an Arab horse. Her parents were both artists, her mother a painter and her father the well-known writer, Ronald Duncan. Both were inspired by the local landscape and its people.

While her parents remained in North Devon, Briony's childhood became peripatetic. When her mother was diagnosed with TB, the child was sent away to boarding school at the age of three. Subsequent interruptions to her education resulted from her parents' fiery and unstable marriage. They sent her at 14 to a convent in France. She returned to Welcombe when she could and happy early memories cluster around its farms, woods and beaches. The chaotic nature of her childhood and education made it difficult for her to settle. It was not until her mid-20s that she began to find her own path in life. She had returned to Welcombe from London where she was making a career for herself in the BBC and begun to help out on her parents' farm. It was hard physical labour that represented a sharp break from her life in London. One day she had the opportunity to attend a pottery class in Bideford, run by Harry Juniper. She made an elephant which is still in her possession. The elephant's feet

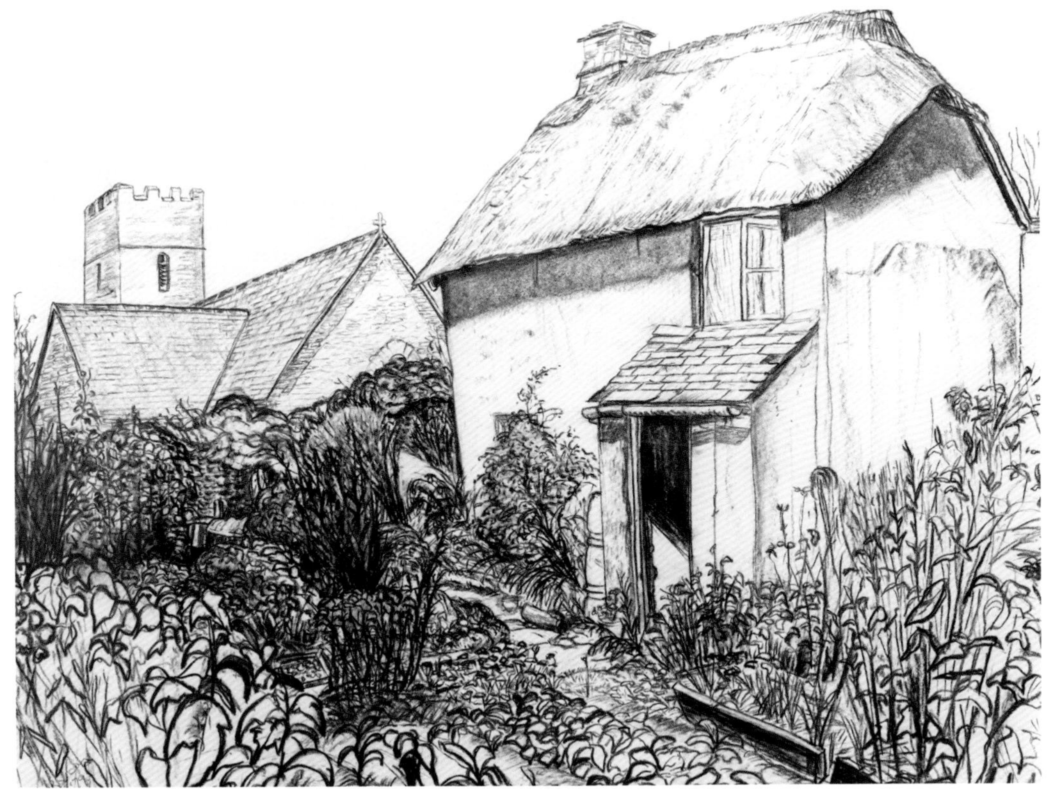

Briony Lawson, *Church Cottage and St Nectan's Church, Welcombe*, 1988. Charcoal

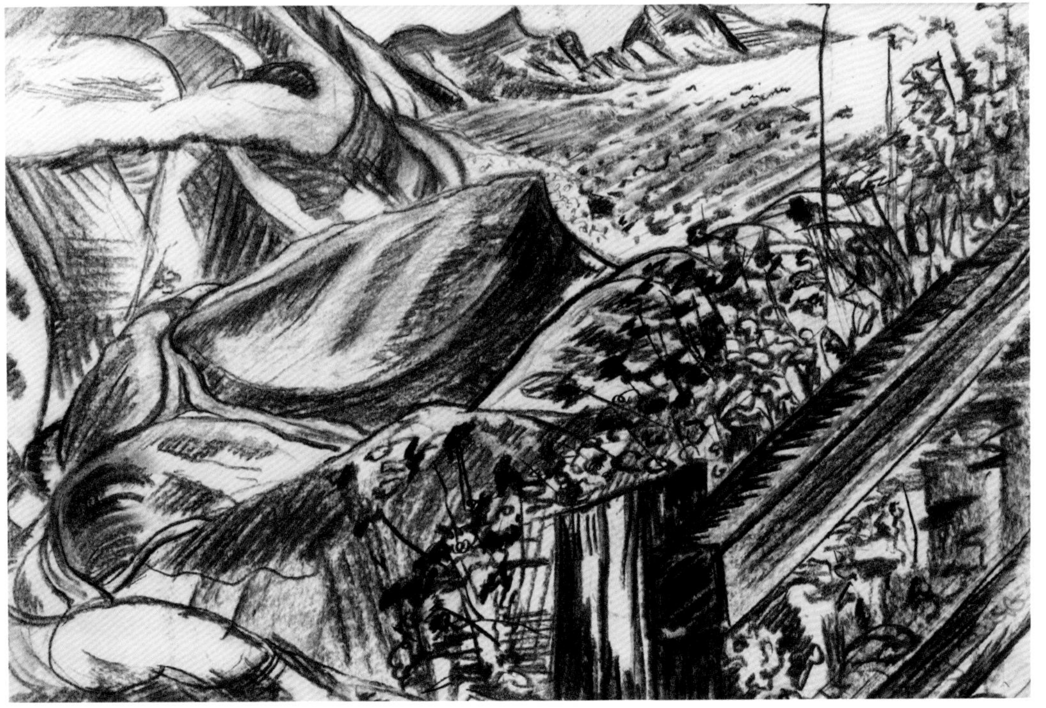

Briony Lawson, *Marsland Coast with Gull Rock*, 2010. Charcoal

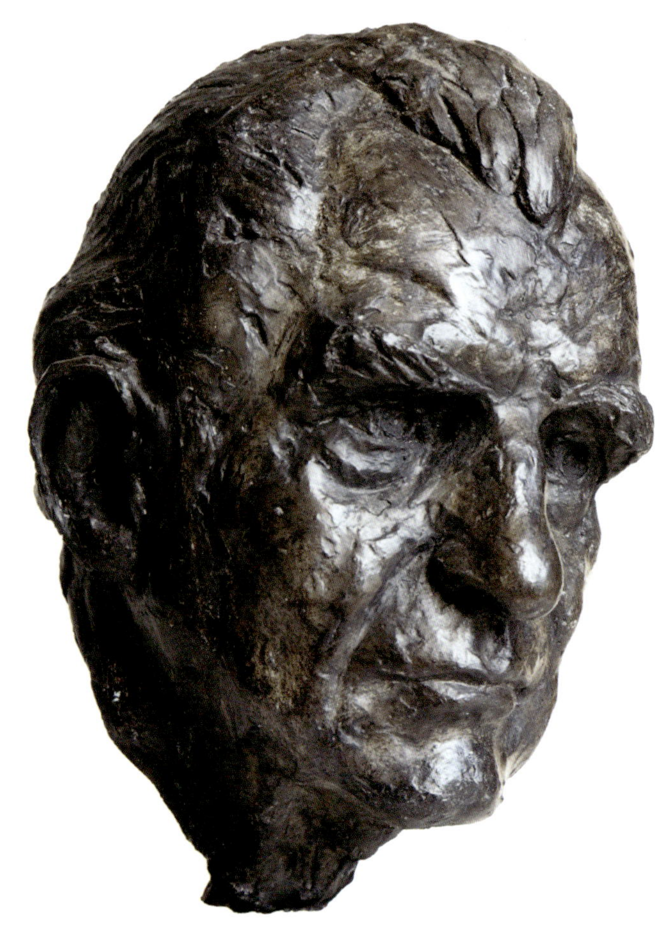

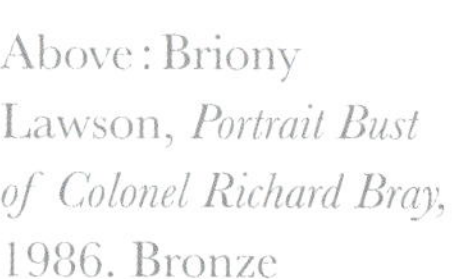

Above: Briony
Lawson, *Portrait Bust
of Colonel Richard Bray*,
1986. Bronze

Right: Briony at
work on clay bust
of Colonel Richard
Bray, 1986

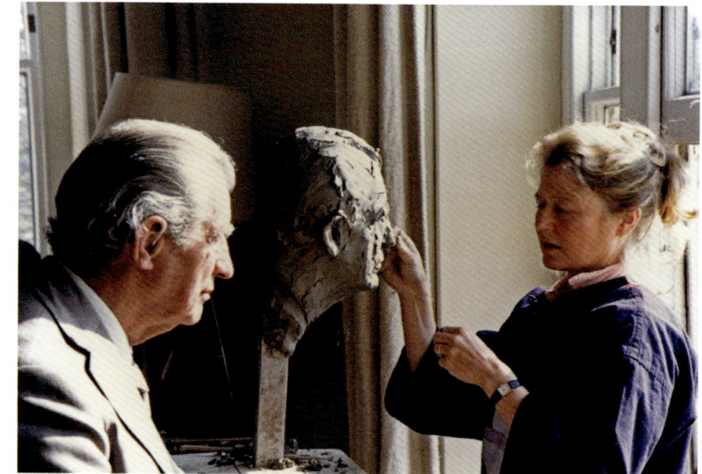

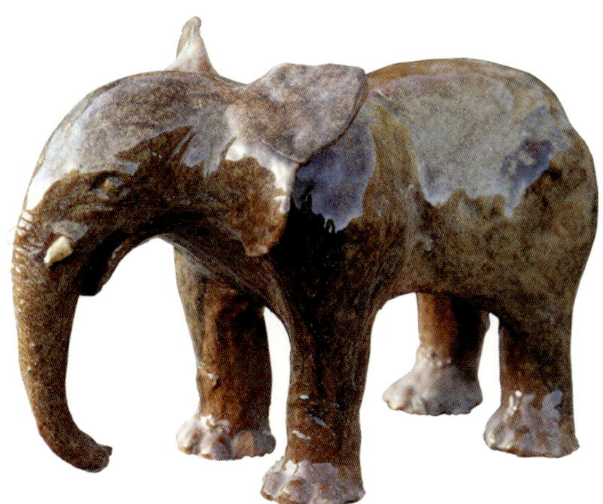

are planted foursquare. It seems to have a great weight and stability which affords protection to the more graceful aspects of the sculpture such as the exaggerated curves of the trunk and tusks. More animals followed and her interest in sculpture grew.

A key moment in her development was seeing 'The Cathedral' by Rodin (she remembers where she was when she saw it in a book; sitting on the kitchen step) and she realised that sculpture was what she wanted to do.

Despite the cerebral aspect of sculpture, the study of aesthetic, historical and social context, it is the physical nature of making that is crucial to Briony – and the fact that she is working with materials which have a direct link to the earth. Rodin's 'The Cathedral' is a complicated work, depicting two right hands not quite touching and the intricate space between them. But in essence it refers to the role of our hands in connecting with each other and with the world. Rodin's work stood out from his contemporaries in that the process of making his work was inseparable from the appearance of the finished piece. The tool marks on "The Cathedral" are not evidence that the sculpture was unfinished but are in keeping with his entire output. It was apparent that it was his hand and brain that determined the form the sculpture took – rather than the anatomy and appearance of his models. This approach stood in opposition to the machine-like finish of other French sculptors of the time whose task was to disguise the nature of the material they worked with and conceal how their sculptures were made.

Having made her decision she plunged into a programme of self-education in her newly chosen profession that saw her attending numerous courses and art schools over the following three years.

She prioritised life drawing and modelling from the figure, slowly building the foundations of her technique (in its broadest sense) before eventually embarking on a full time course at City and Guilds Art School. She was one of only three sculpture students and took advantage of all the facilities on offer. These included enrolling on a course in restoration to discover more about older ways of working.

It was while she was in London that she met Andrew Lawson – who was finishing his studies at St Martins – and who began to help her with her work – the beginning of a lifetime's pursuit together.

Over the years Briony has explored the properties of her chosen materials – wood, stone and clay. Clay, being the most flexible material has produced the most diverse results while the discipline of carving has produced a steady exploration of the possibilities lurking within tree trunk and block. Her wood carvings in particular are a dialogue between herself and her material – the nature of the particular kind of wood she is using, the grain and its original shape – seems to fashion her sculptures, as if Briony is allowing the wood to take on the form it desires. I started here by mentioning Moore and Rodin yet probably the greatest influence on her work has been Brancusi. Brancusi is famous for his pursuit of simplicity, his continual distillation of life's richness and complexity into essence. Briony's sculpture works towards simplicity and essence as a means of mending and renewal; wiping away the surplus accretions of life in order to return to something that lies at her core.

Briony sometimes refers to her lack of education while she was growing up – which she has striven to rectify throughout her life. But it is perhaps significant that her two greatest influences, Rodin and Brancusi are distinguished by their lack of formal education or apprenticeships. These hindrances they transformed into advantages through nurturing self-reliance and an independence of thought.

Looking at her wooden sculptures based on the ferns that abound throughout Marsland, I can see how her work connects with the landscape – and as I glance from the waving grass and wind tossed branches to her rippling shapes – I swear I can see her sculptures move.

14

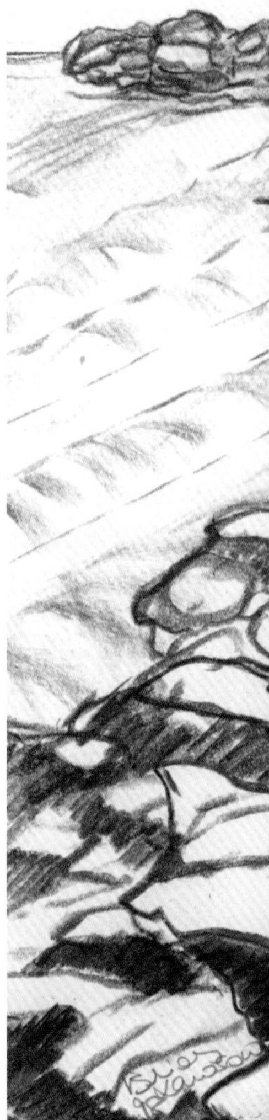

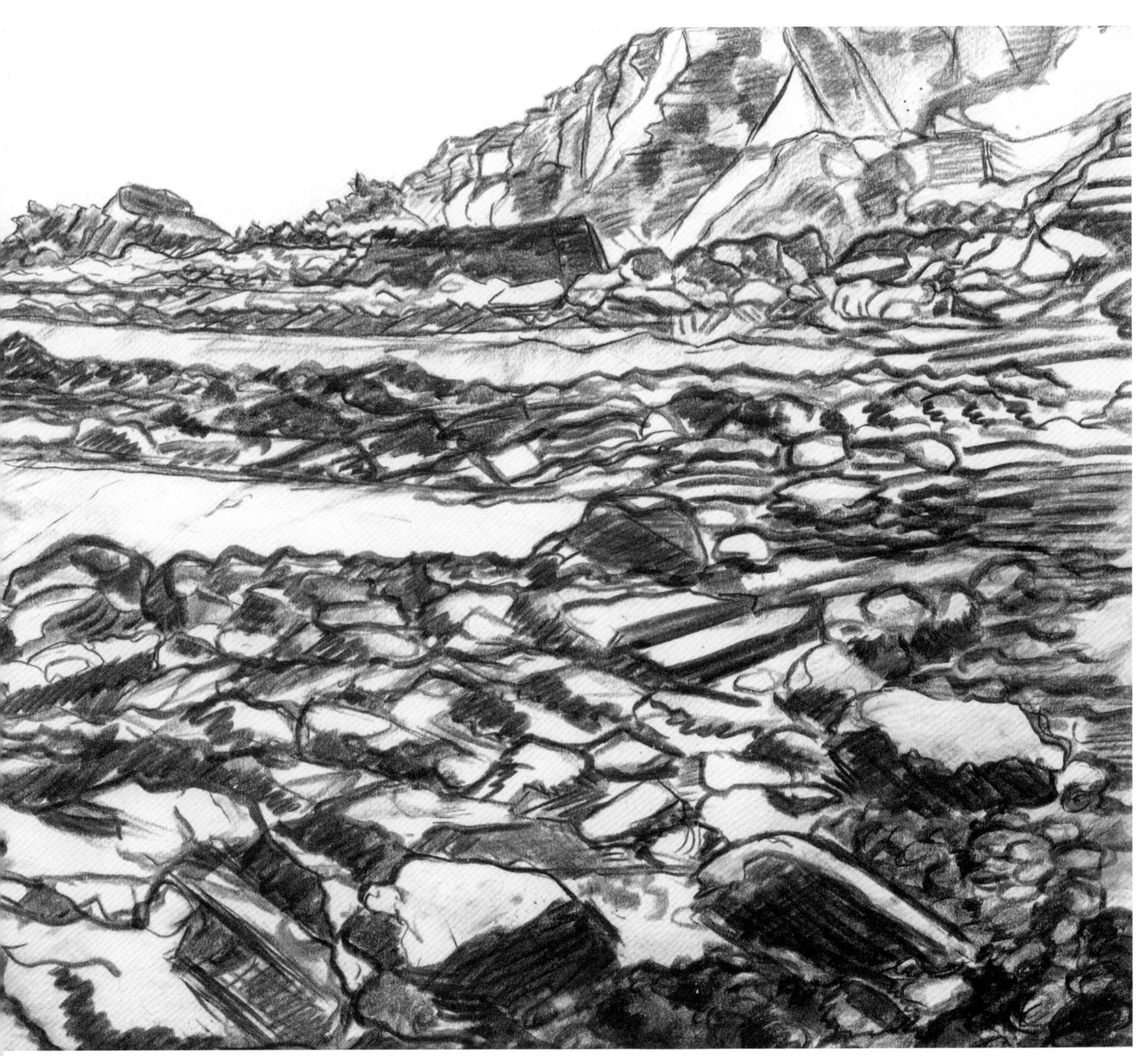

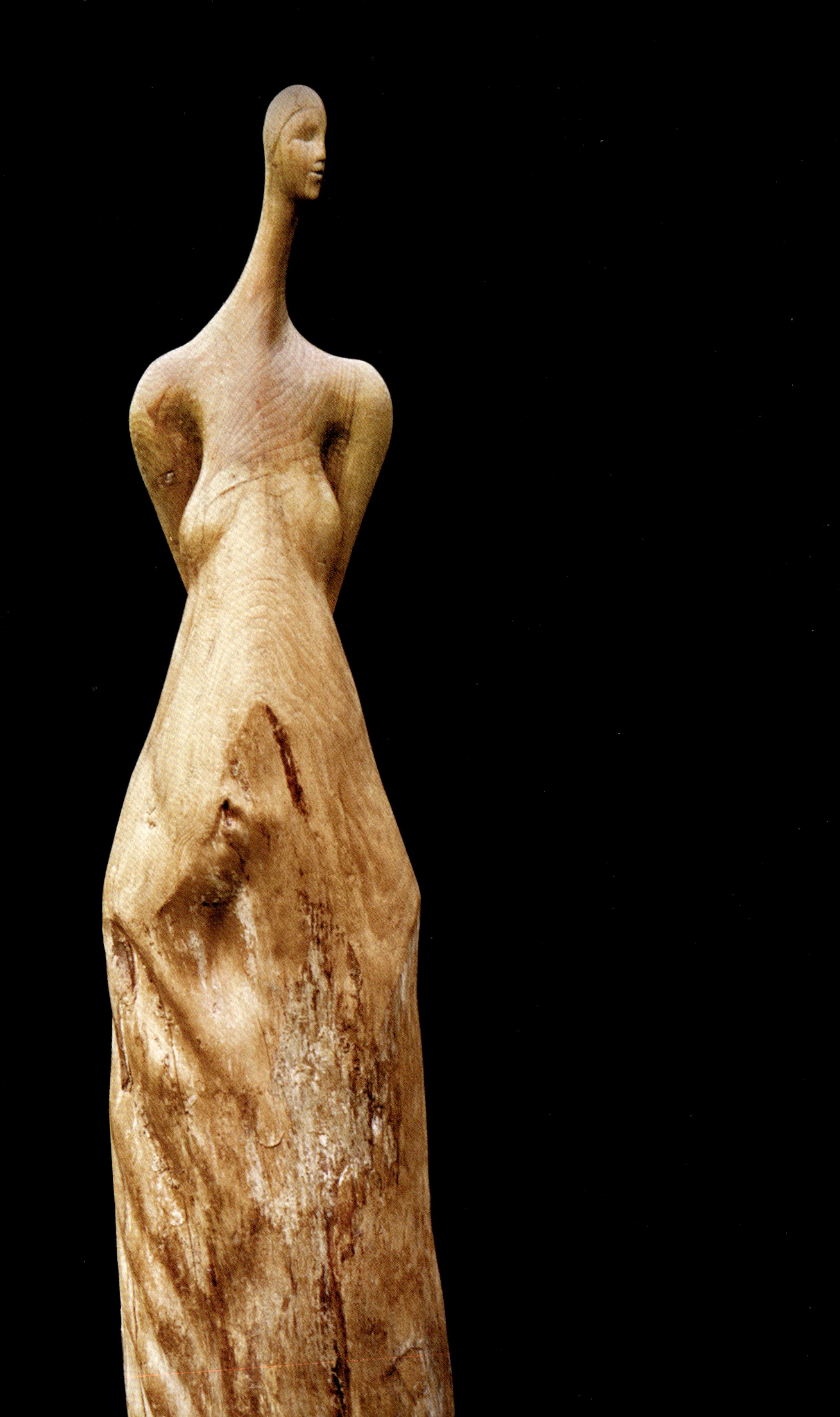

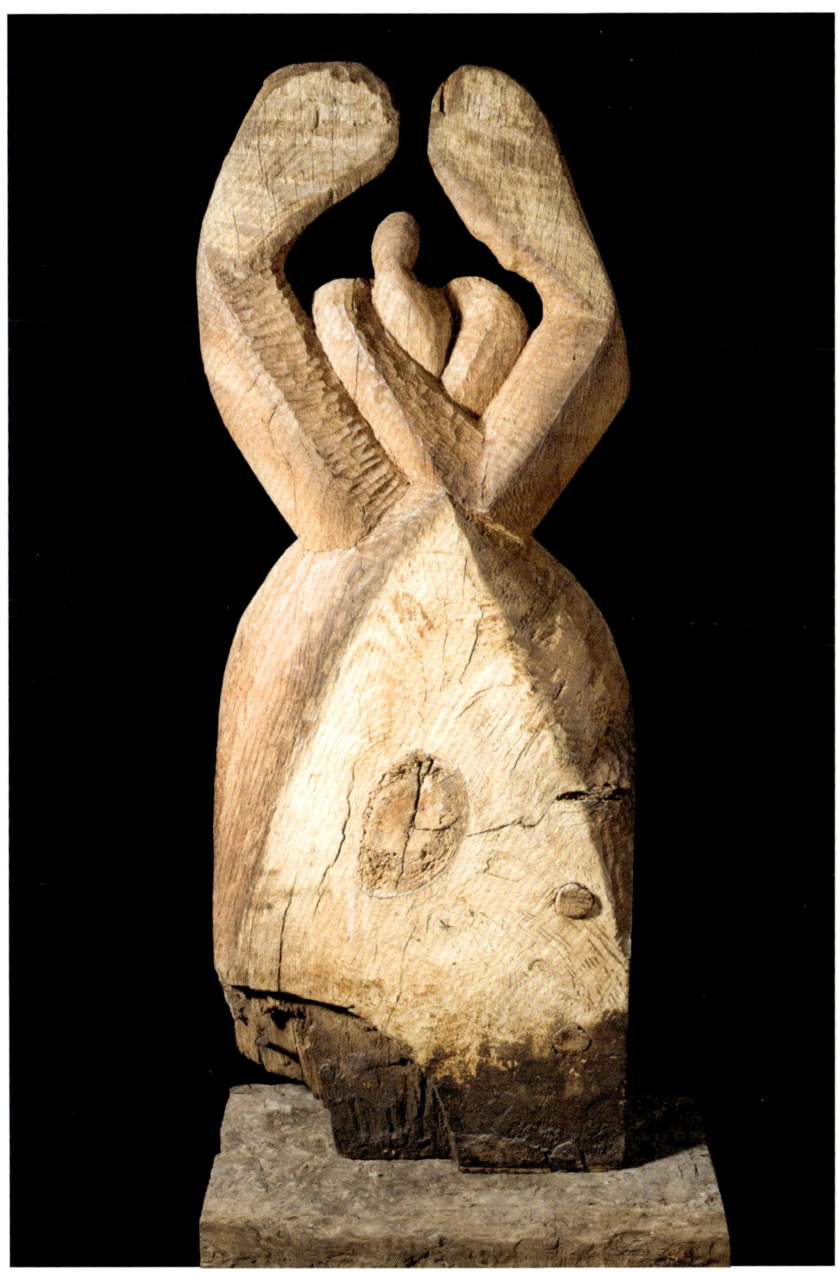

like to work with old
wood. Salvaged oak
beams are the ideal
material for me. I try to
respect the particular
character of each piece
of wood and aim to
retain some of its history
in the final work."

Left: Briony Lawson,
The Family, 2009.
Oak

Far Left: Briony
Lawson, *Maternity*,
1985. Yew

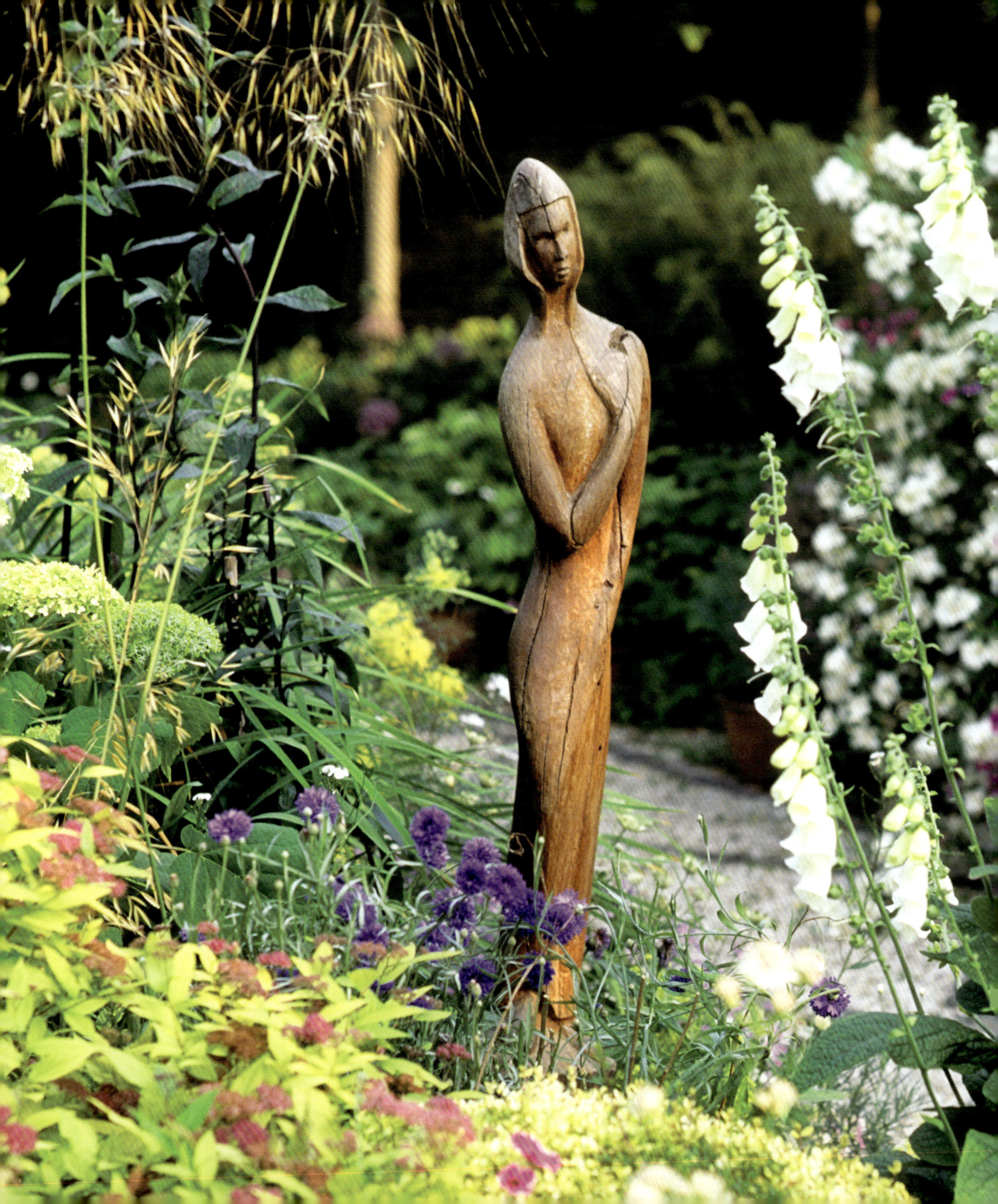

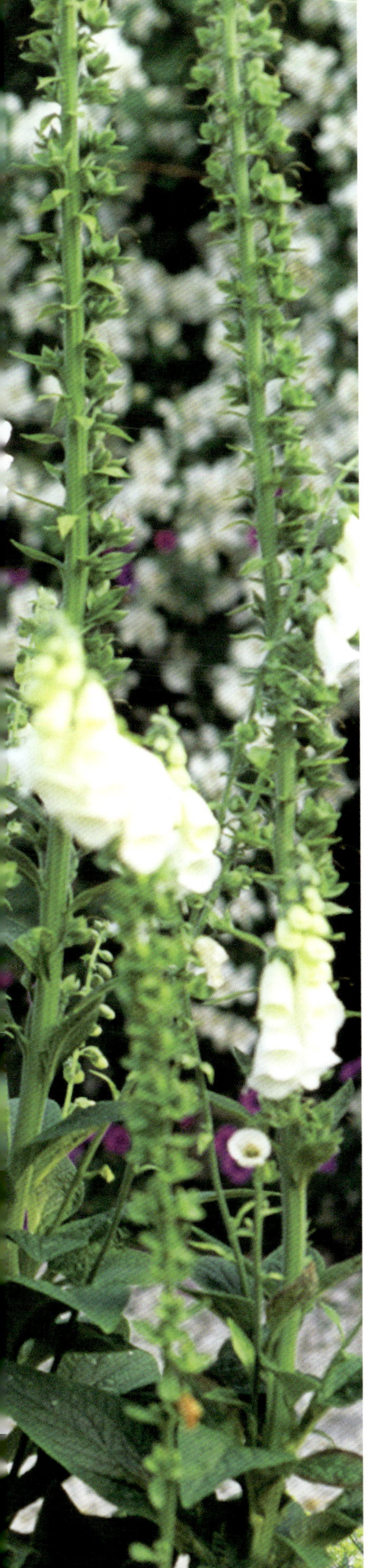

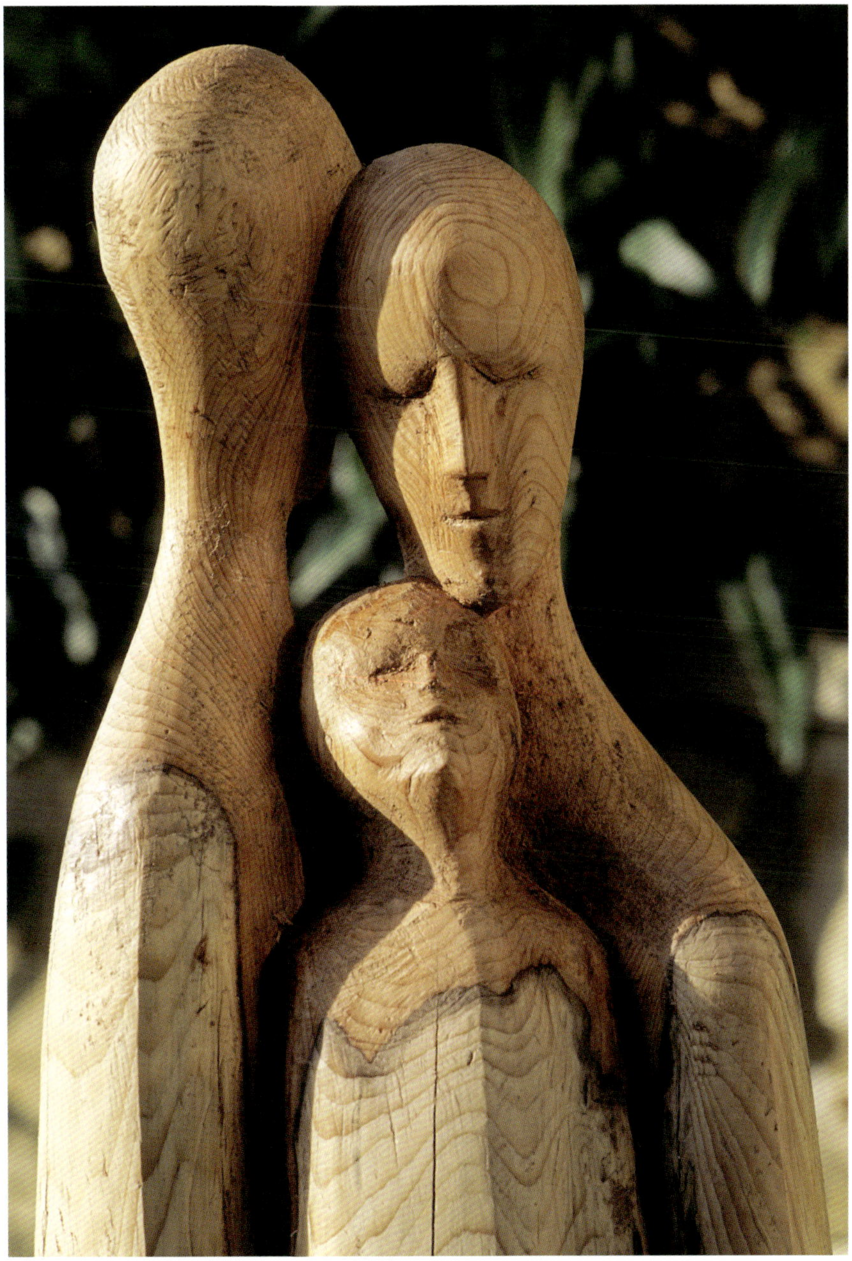

Left: Briony Lawson,
The Pilgrim, 1977. Oak,
set in the garden at
Gothic House

Above: Briony Lawson,
Family Group, 2002. Yew

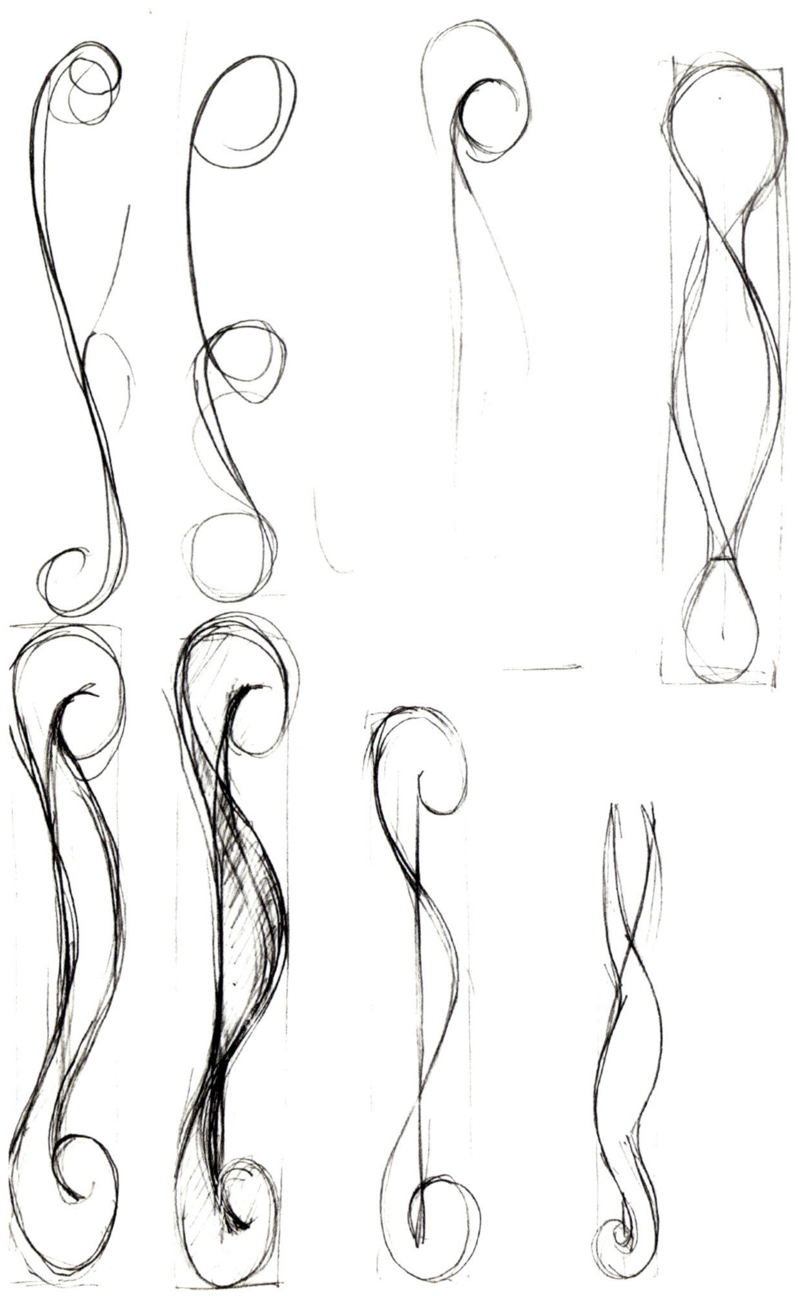

Briony Lawson, *Working Drawings*, 1976. Pencil

Right: Briony Lawson, *Fern Series*, 2009–2010. Oak

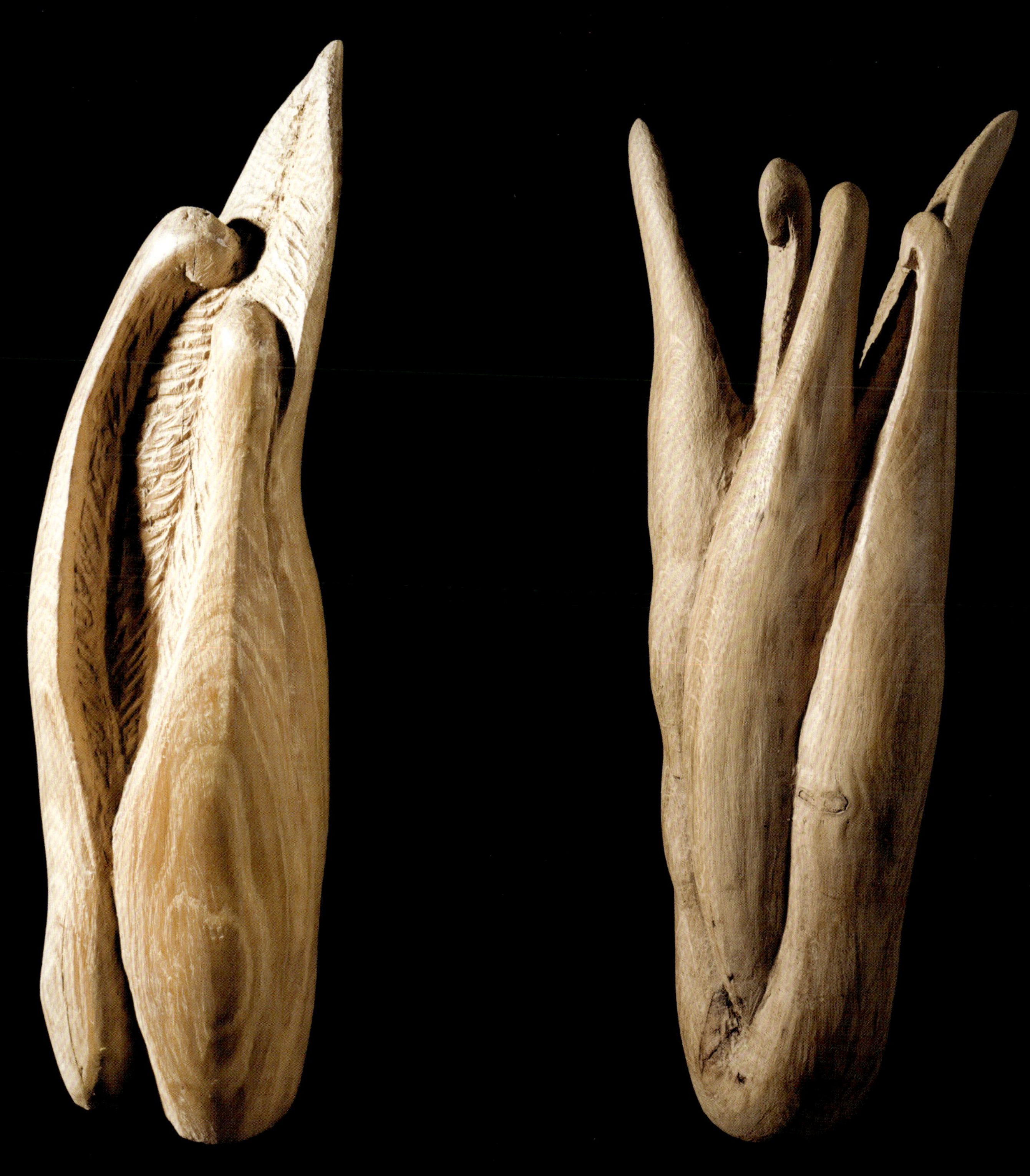

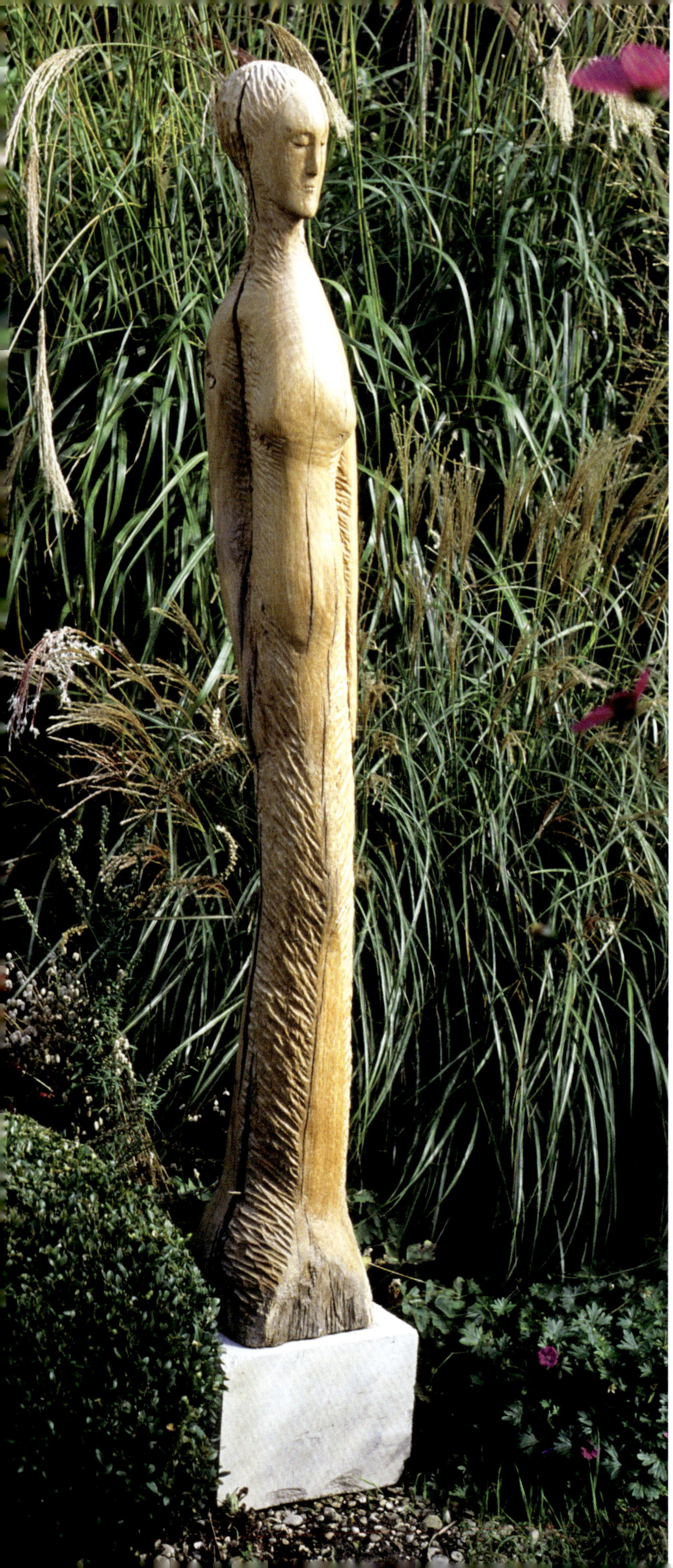

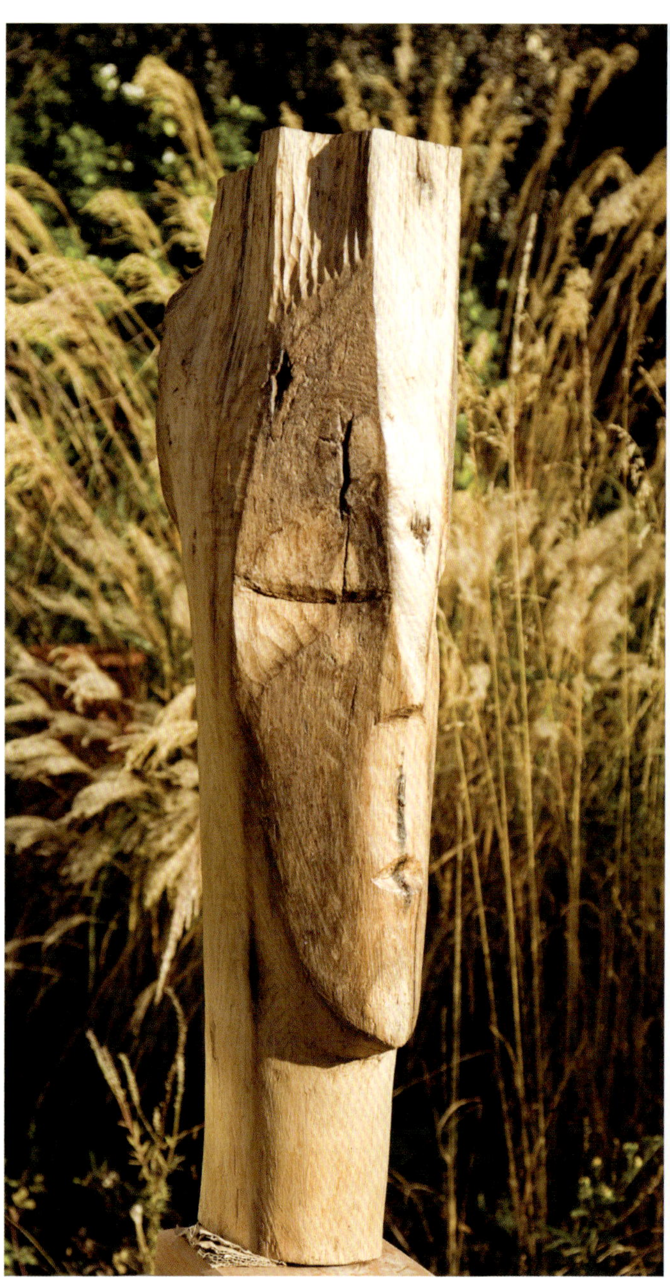

Left : Briony Lawson,
Electra, 2003. Oak

Right : Briony
Lawson, *Three Kings* :
*Melchior, Caspar,
Balthazar*, 2010. Oak

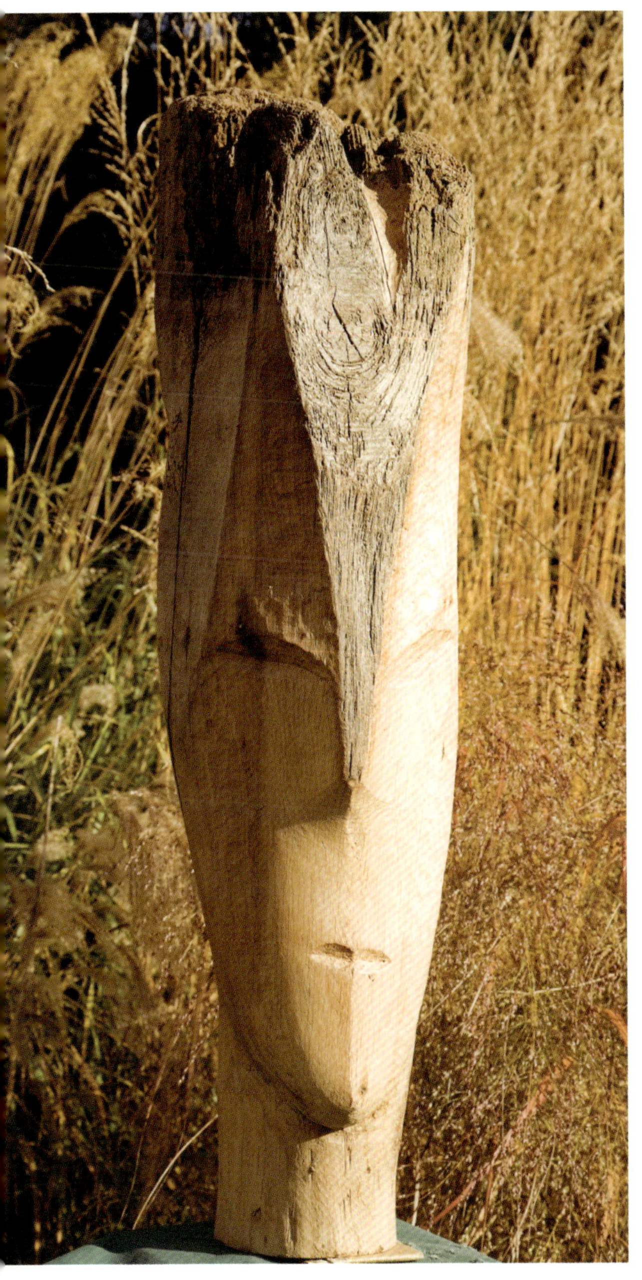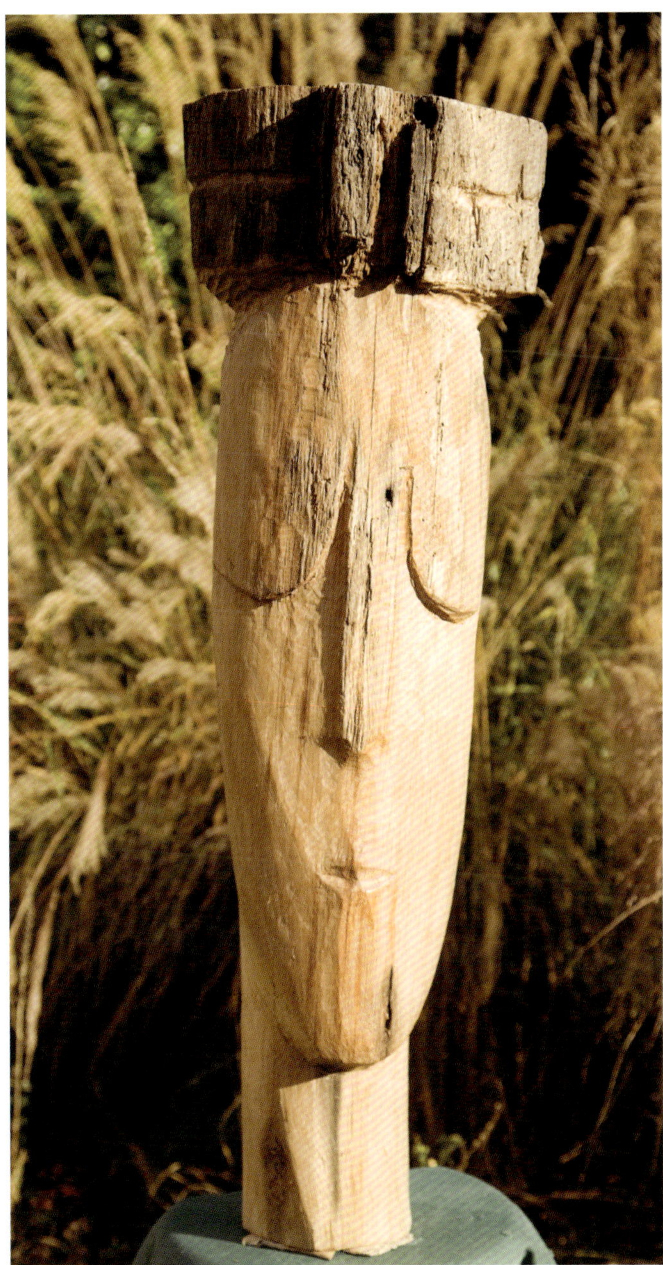

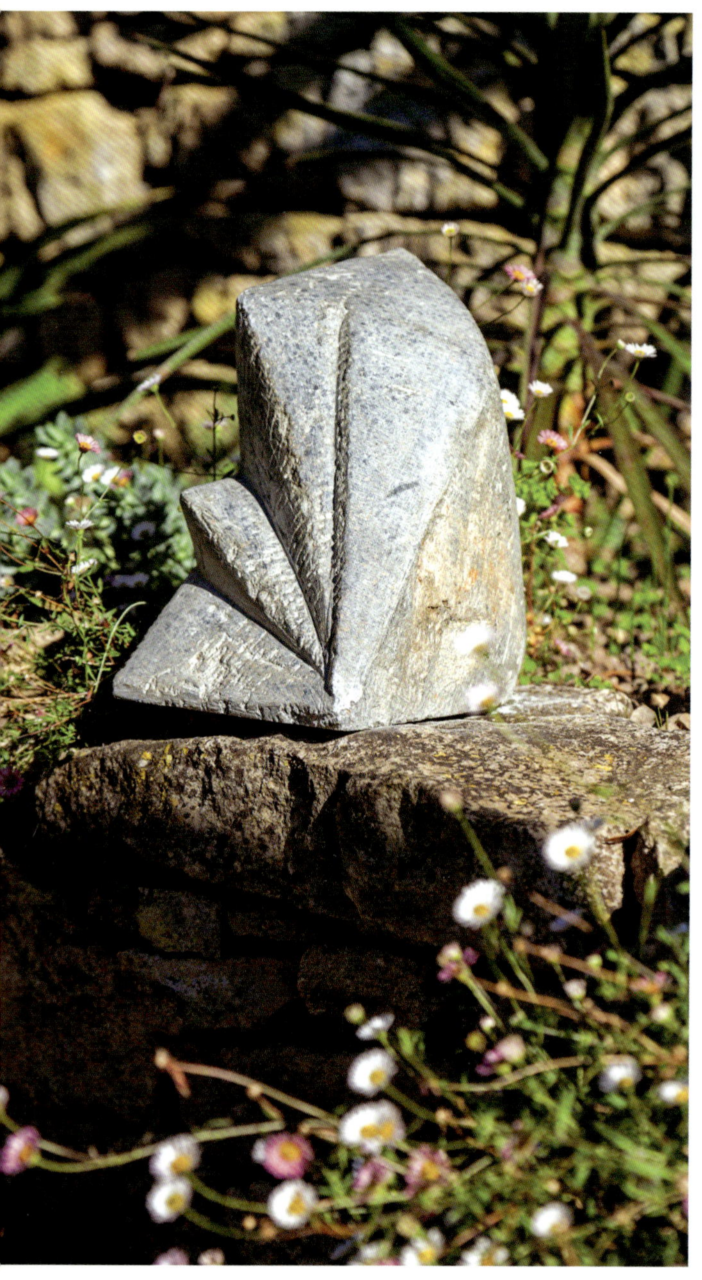

Briony Lawson,
*Landscape Form : Jagged
Cliff*, 2009. Soapstone

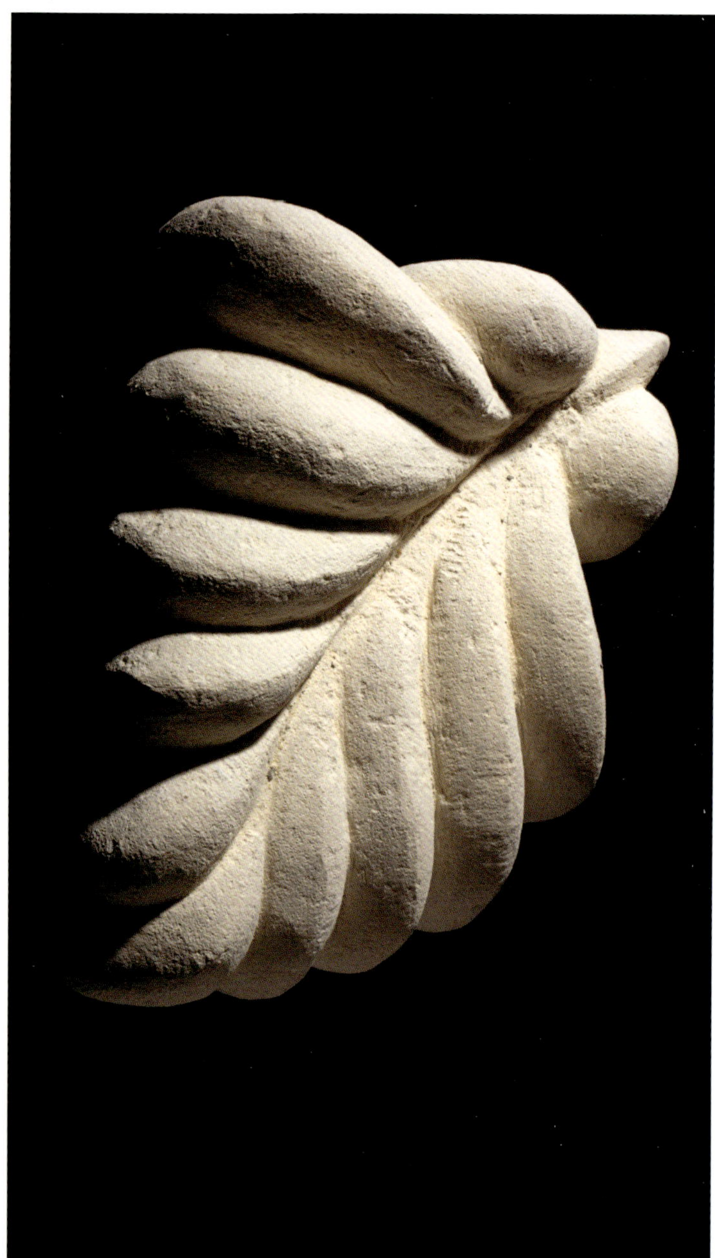

Briony Lawson, *Leaf
Form*, 2008. Portland
Limestone

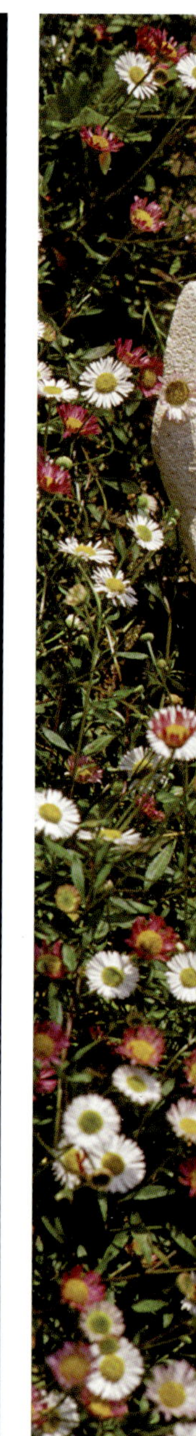

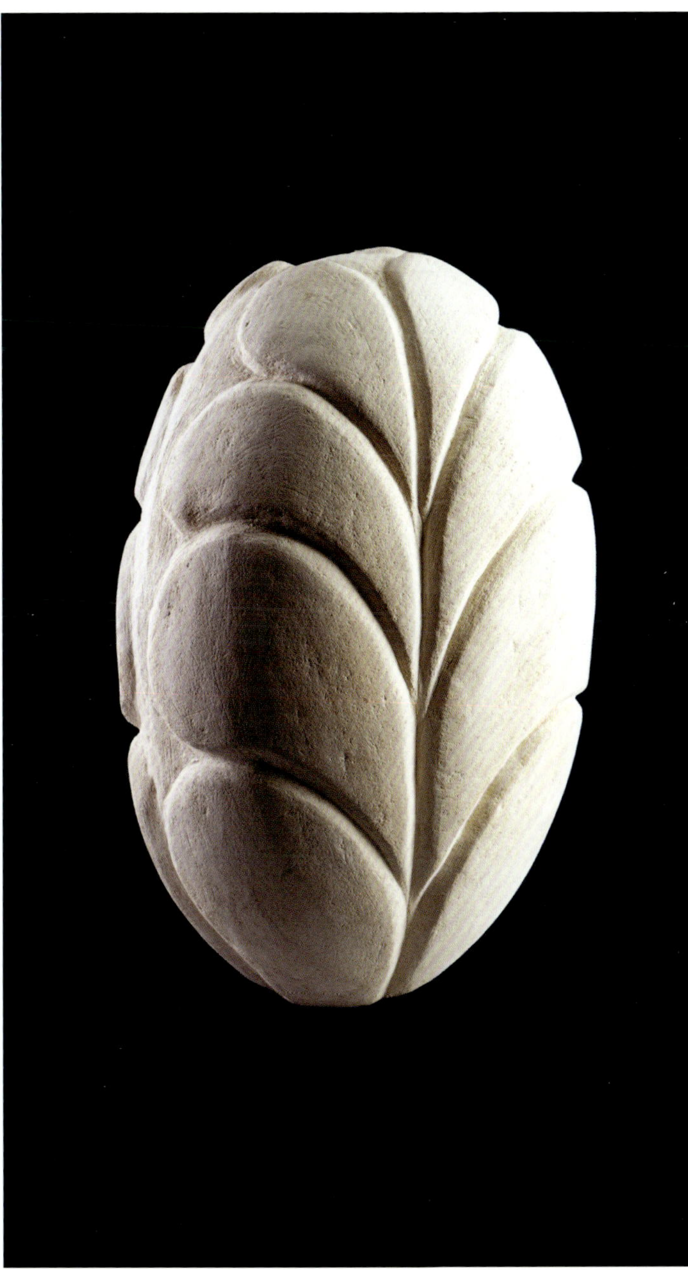

Stone

"Stone is the hardest and most intractable material for sculpture. Its fine grain allows detailed work and enables a contrast between rough and smooth finishes."

Briony Lawson,
Leaf Form, 2008.
Limestone

Briony Lawson, *Plant
Form*, 2016. Portland
Limestone

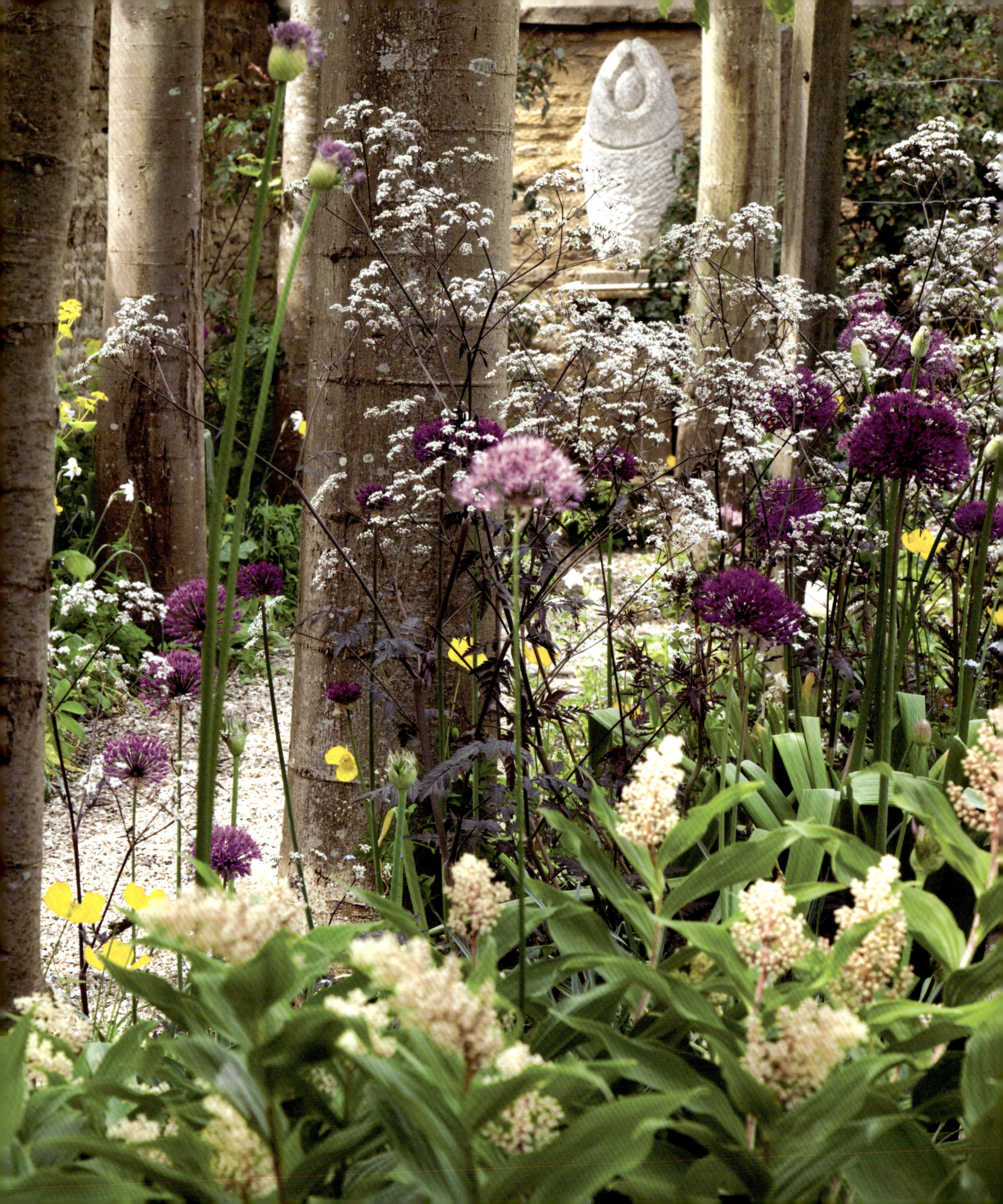

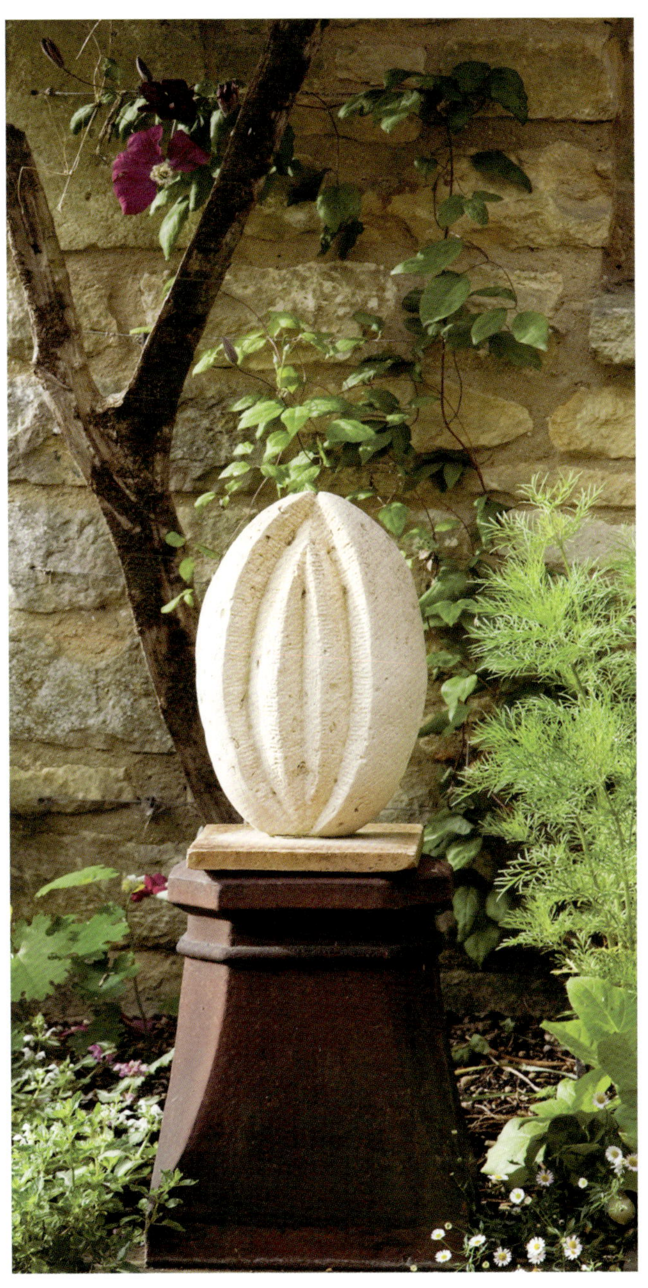

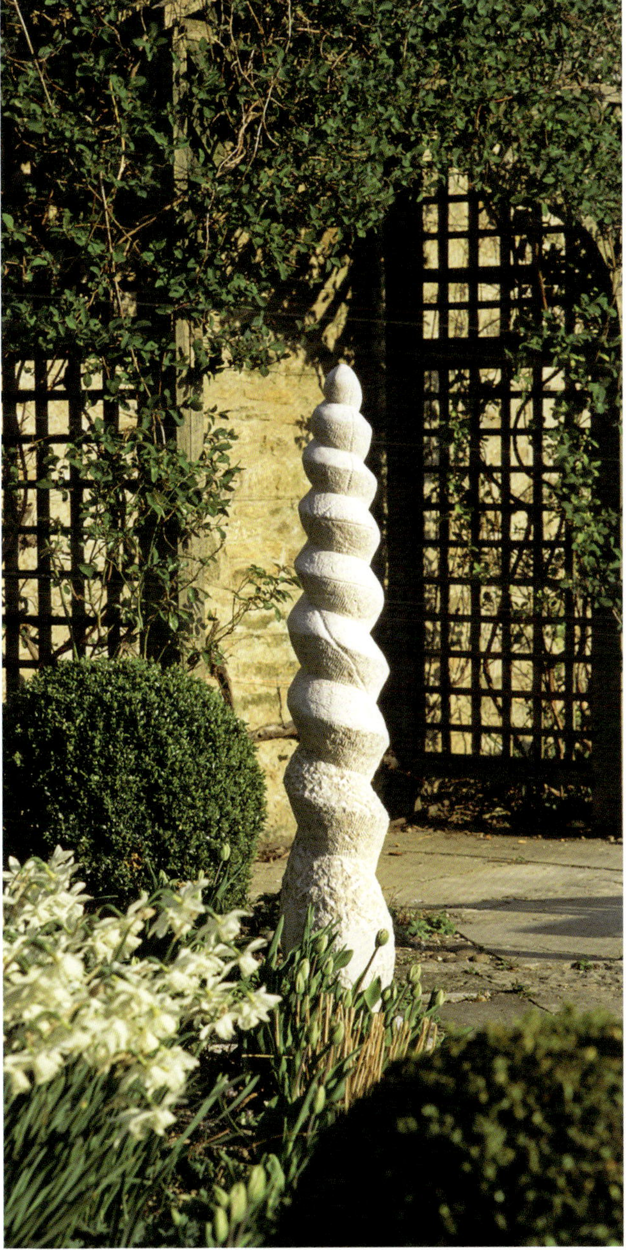

Left : Briony Lawson,
Collared Bud, 1997.
Portland Limestone,
set in the garden at
Gothic House

Above : Briony
Lawson, *Bud Form*,
1997. Limestone

Briony Lawson, *Spiral
Form*, 1998. Portland
Limestone

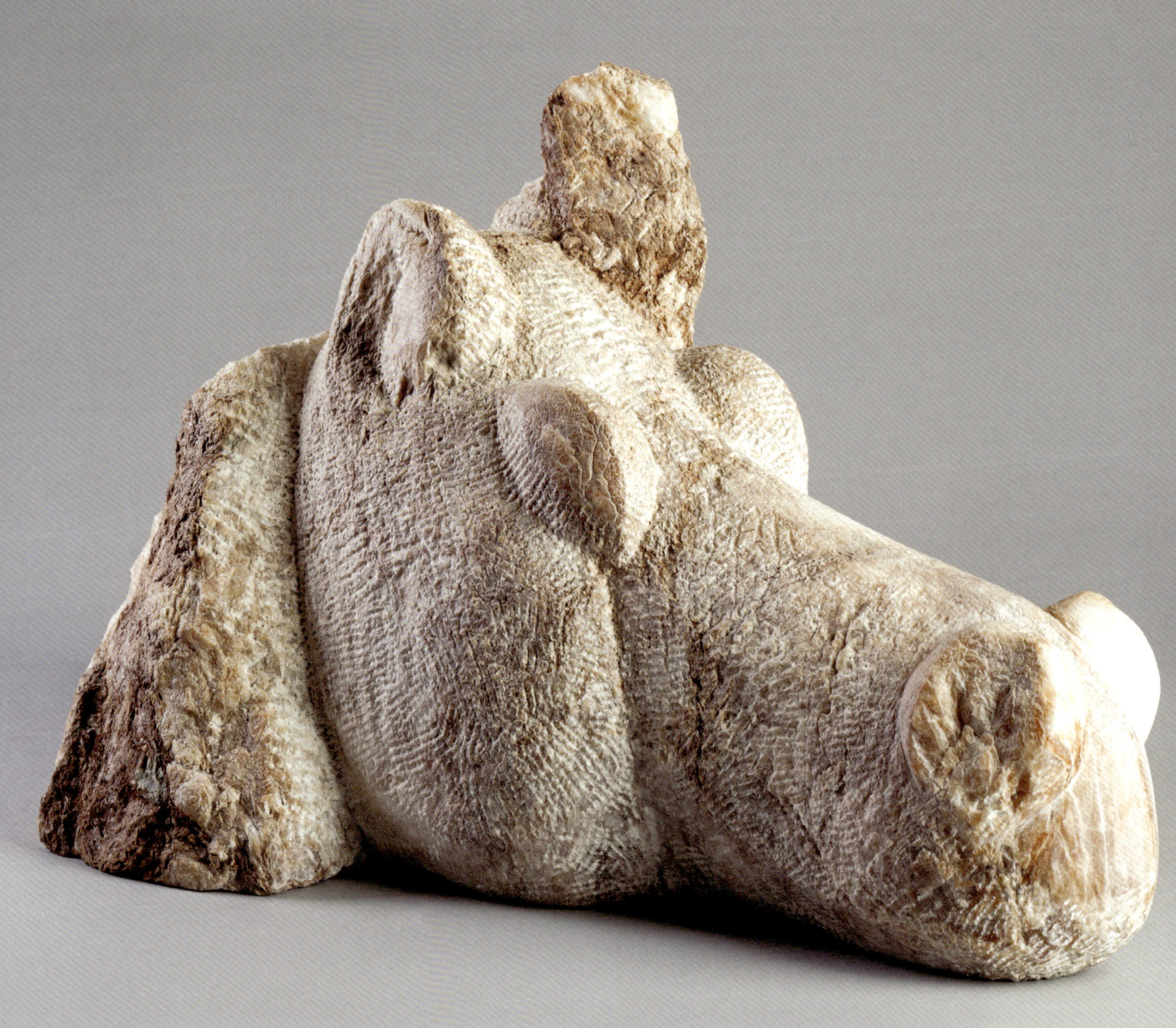

Left : Briony Lawson,
Pegasus, 2003.
Alabaster

Right : Briony
Lawson, *Karina
Sleeping*, 1980. Marble

Right Below : Briony
Lawson, *Daphne*,
2011. Soapstone

Far Right : Briony
Lawson, *Aglaia*, 2017.
Soapstone

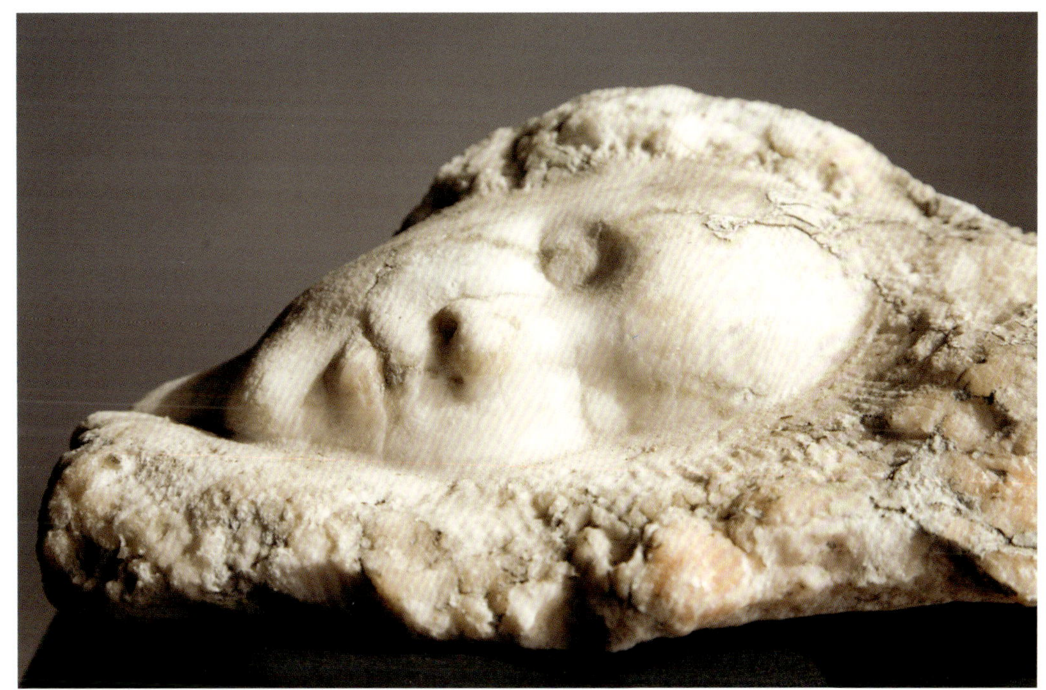

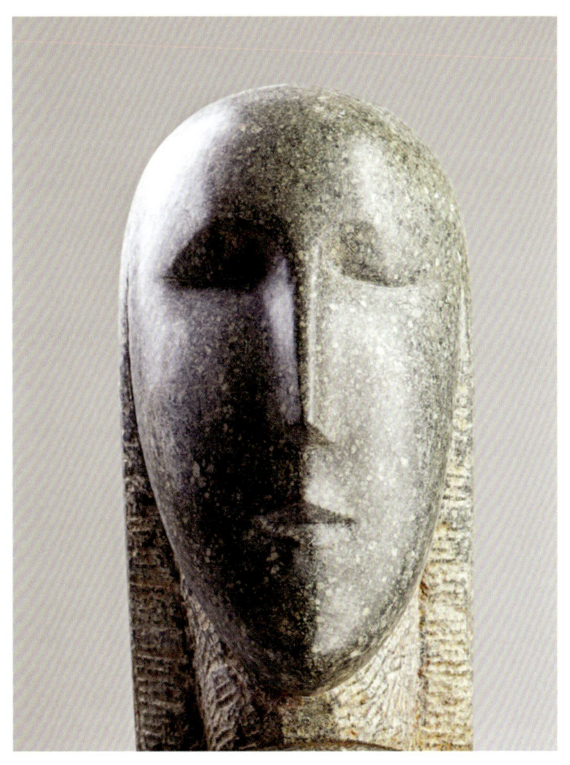

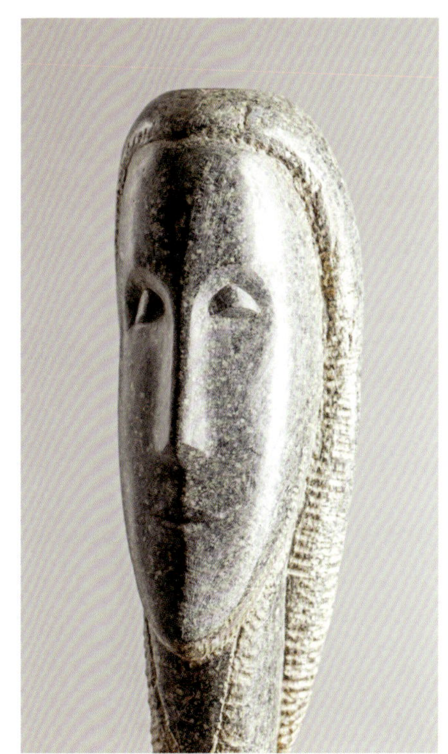

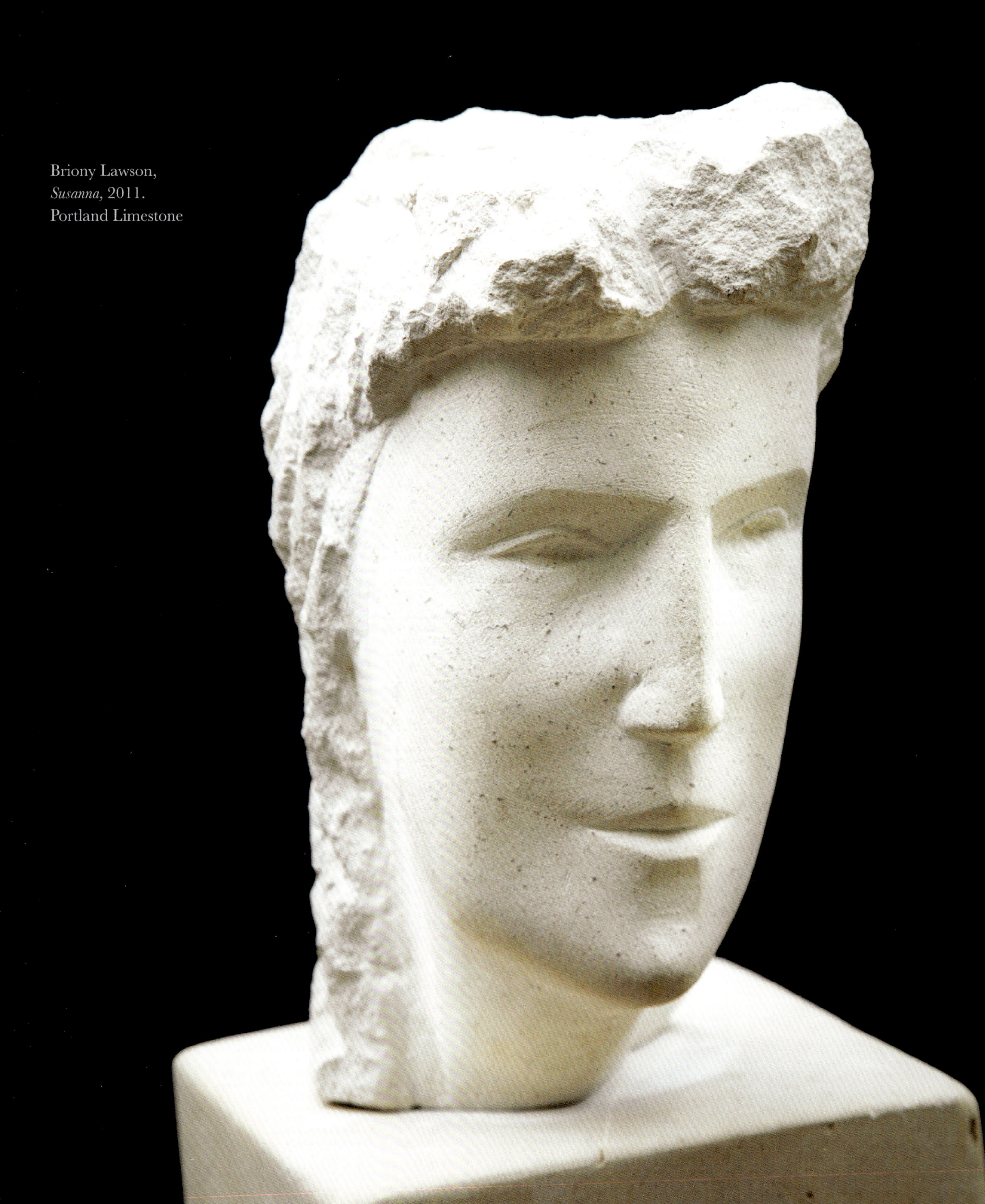

Briony Lawson,
Susanna, 2011.
Portland Limestone

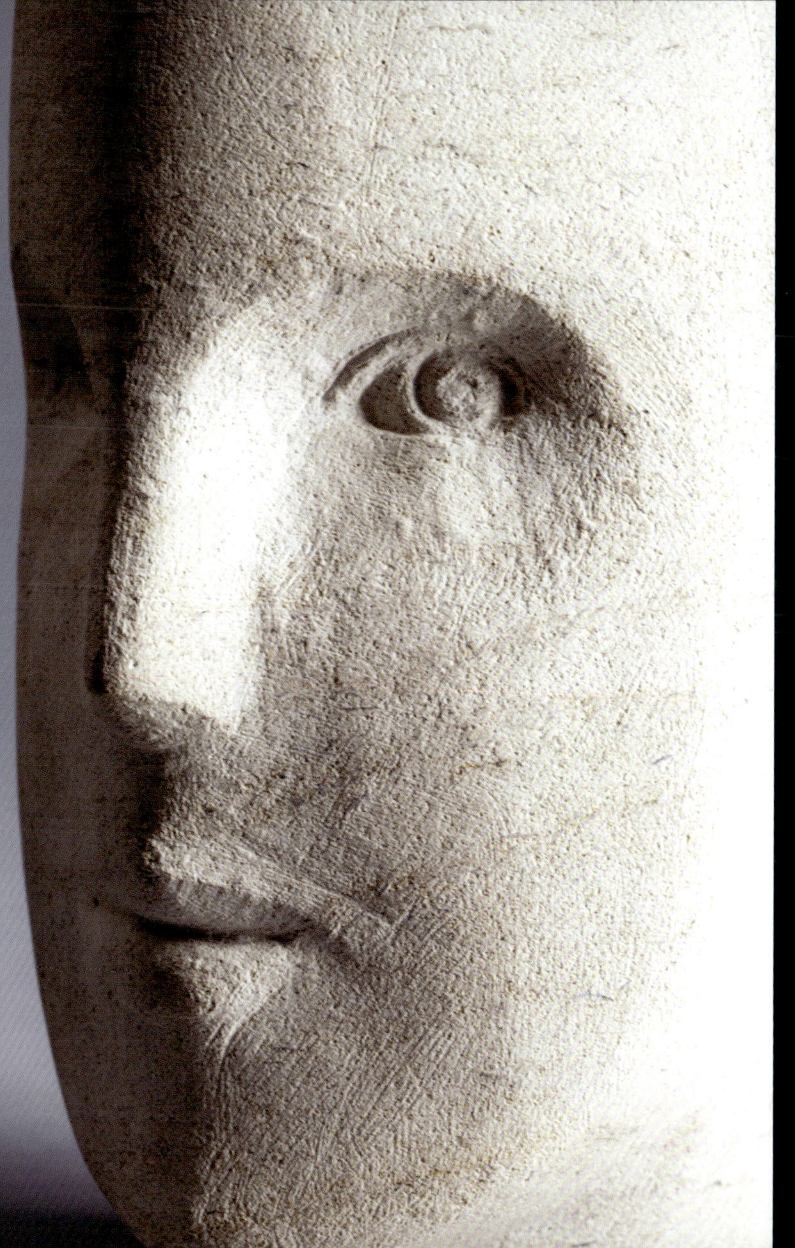

Briony Lawson.
Sacha, 2017.
Limestone

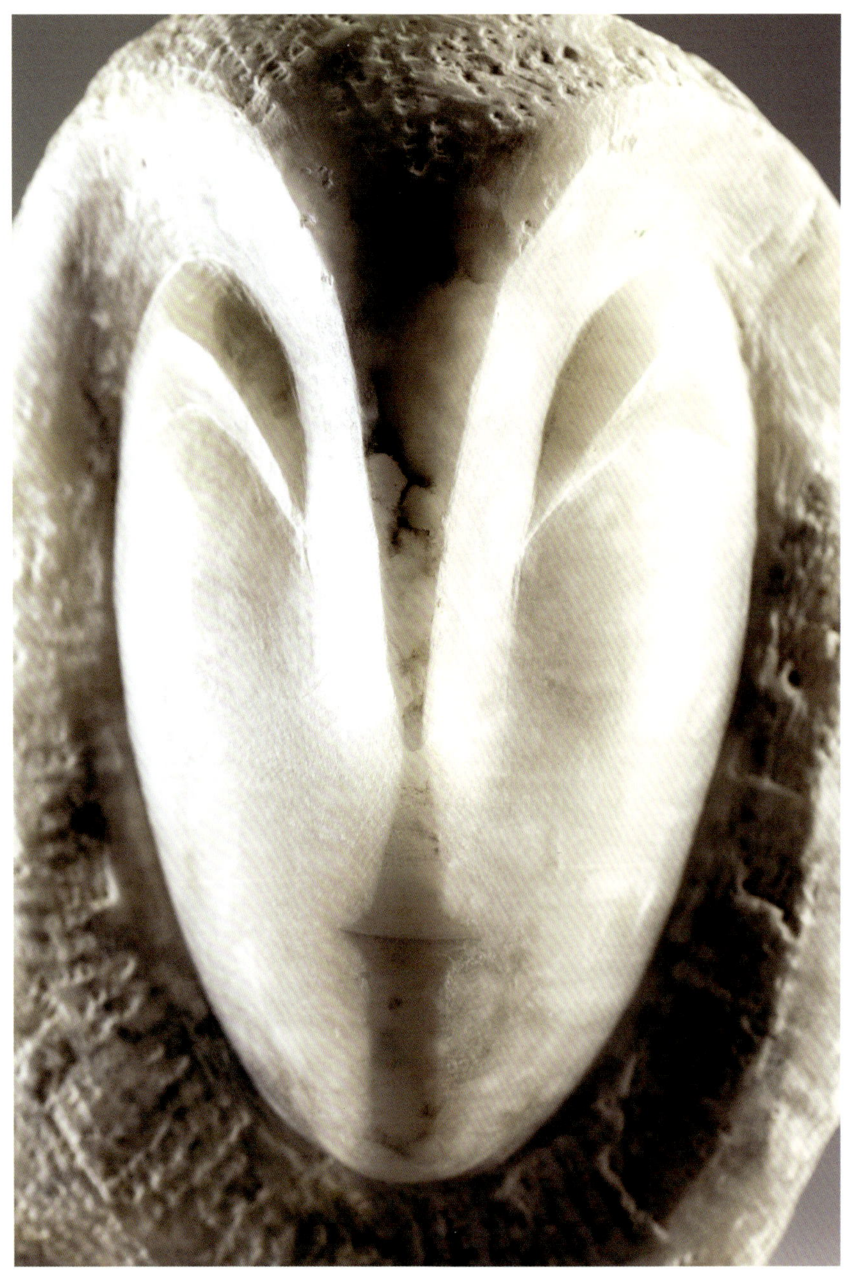

Right : Briony Lawson,
Xenia, 2017. Portland
Limestone

Briony Lawson ,
Athena, 2011.
Alabaster

32

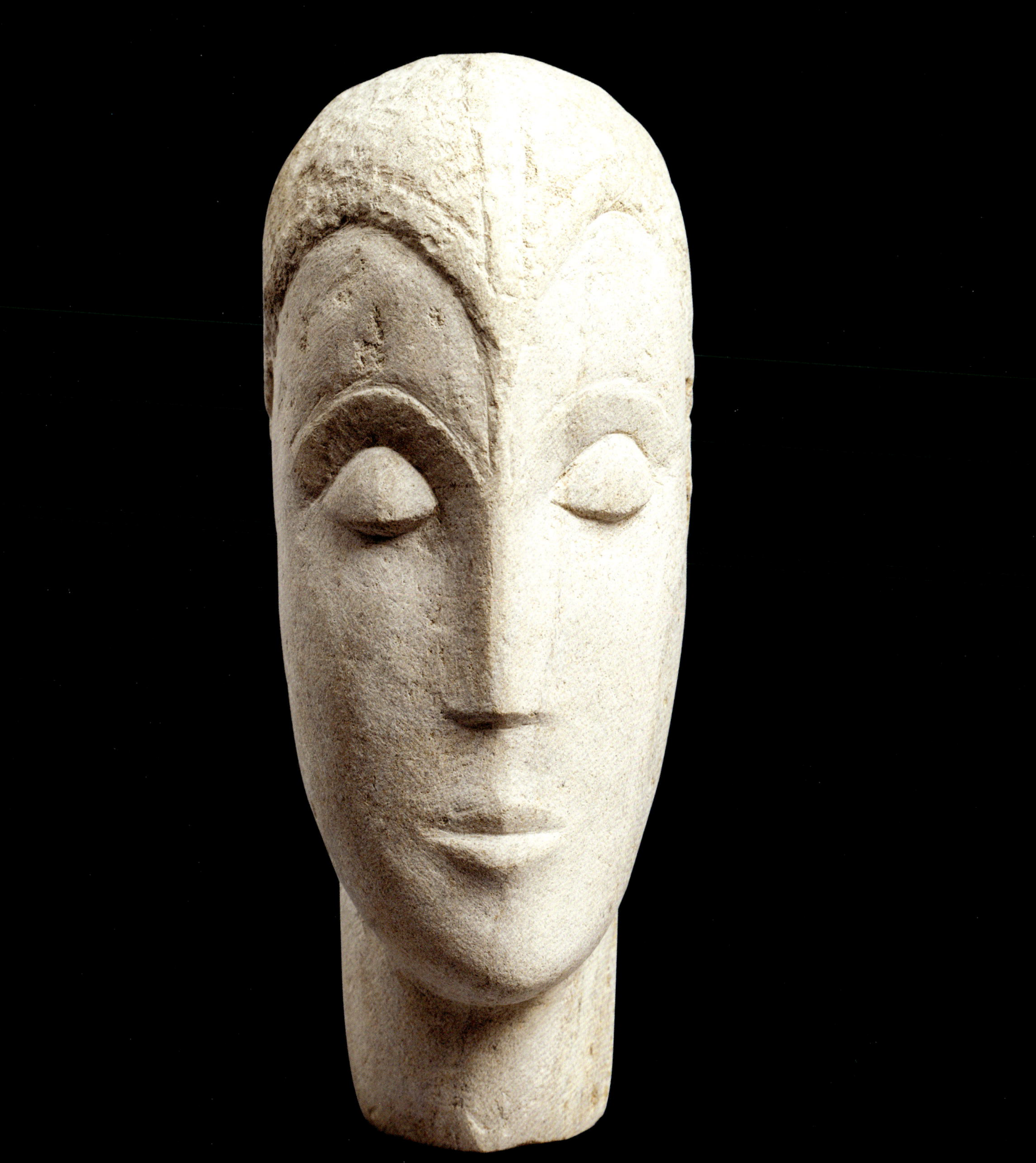

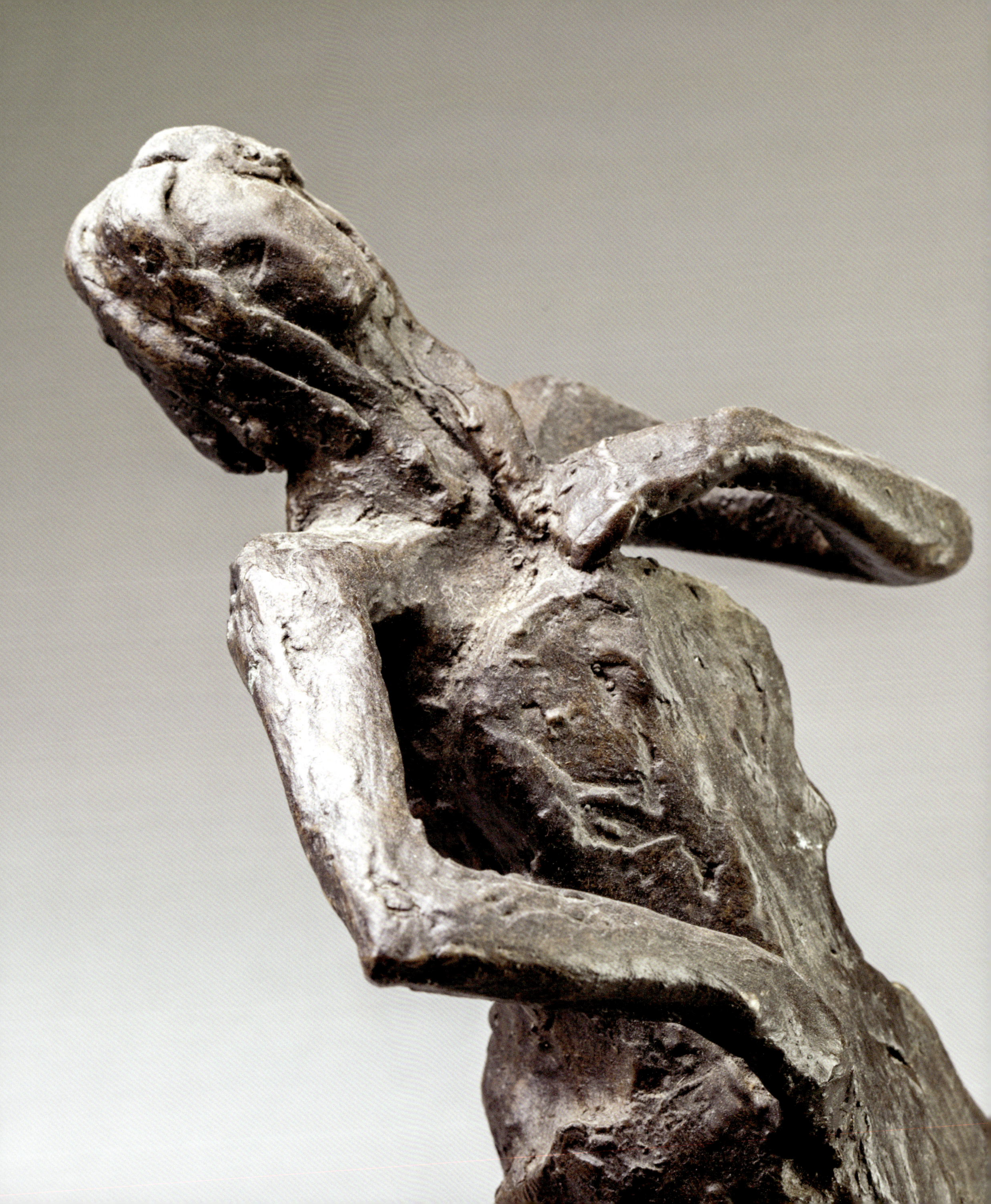

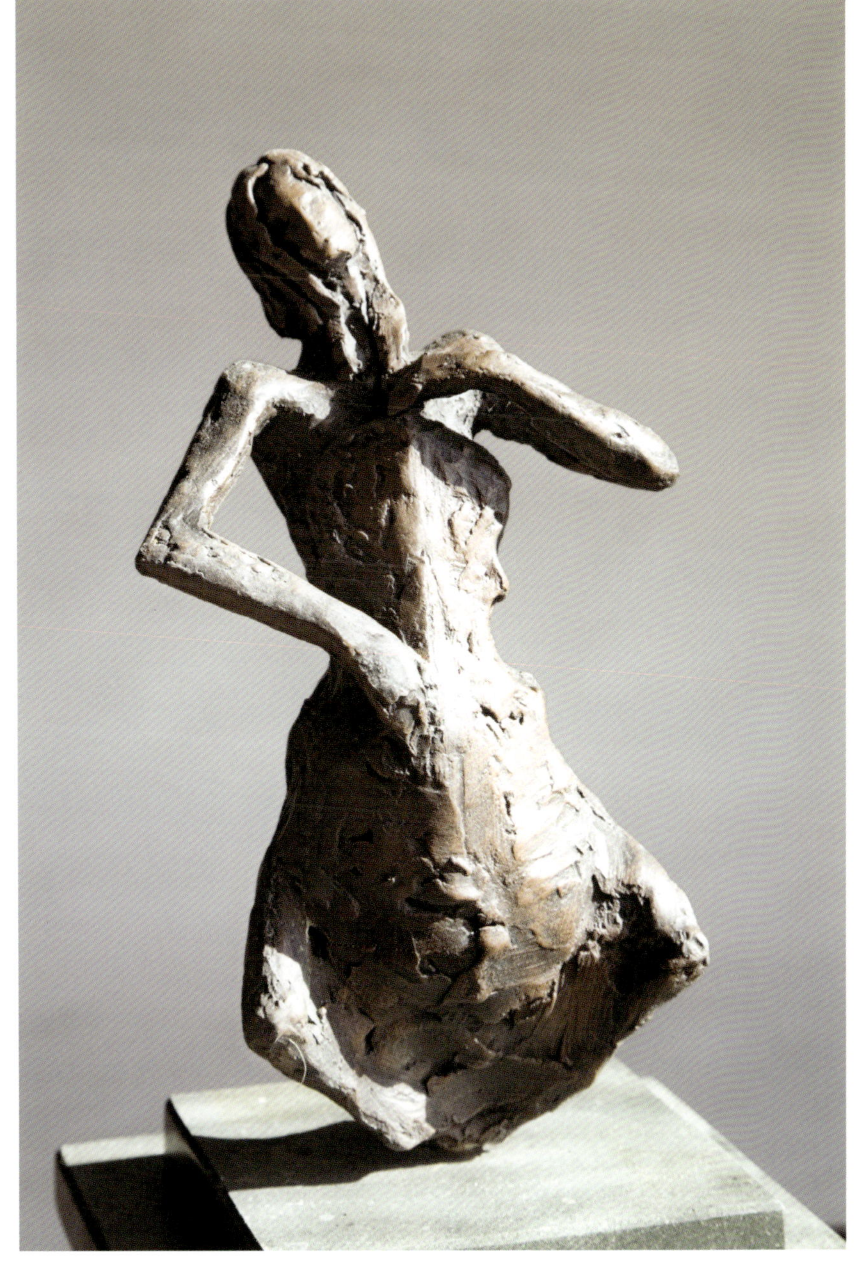

Modelling with clay is the most frec of all the mediums. You can build up the forms but also cut back through them by carving. Clay is a fragile material and the finished sculpture needs to be fired as terracotta or cast in bronze or resin."

Left and Far Left: Briony Lawson, *The Cellist (Jacqueline du Pré)*, 1998. Copper Resin

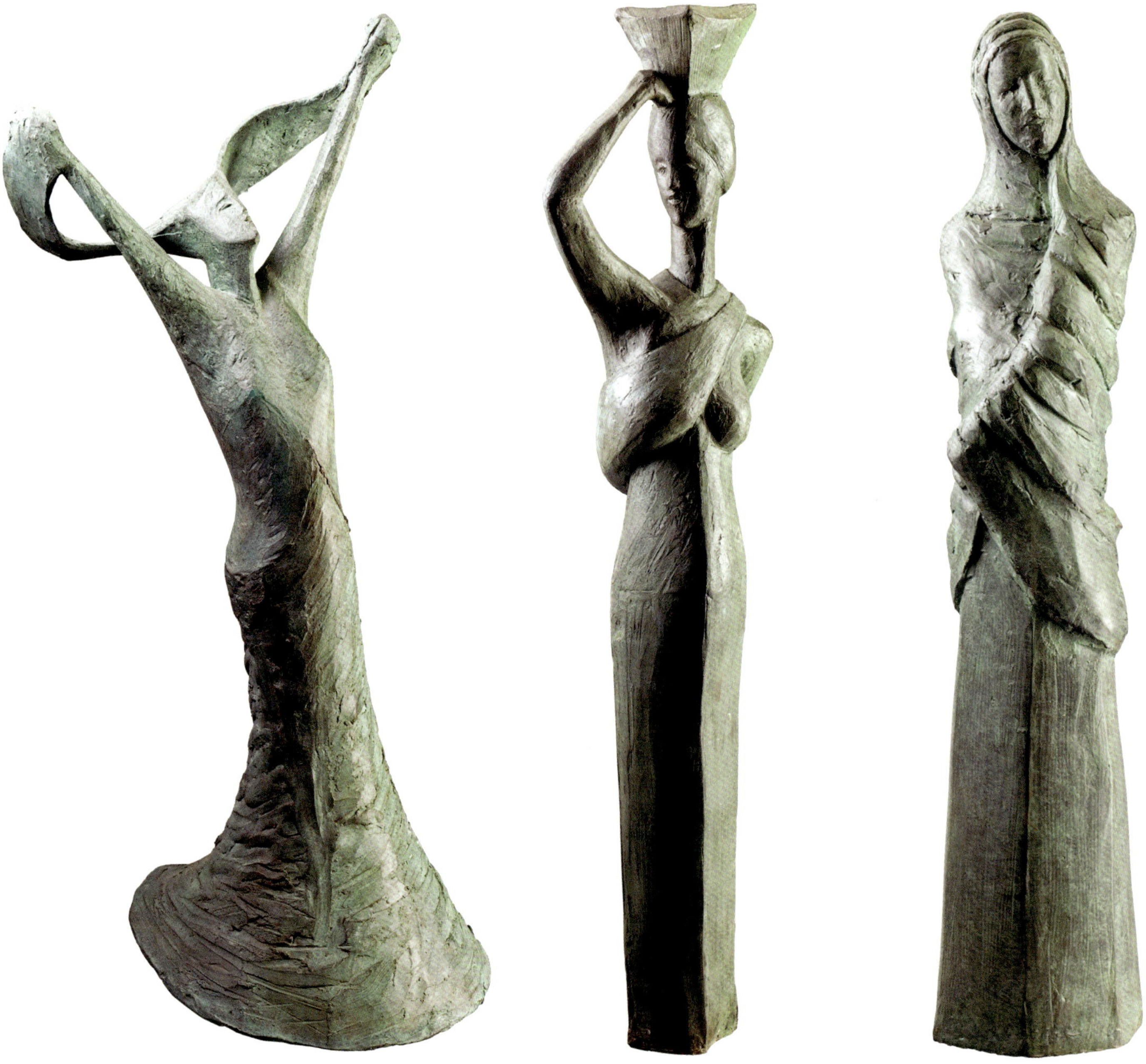

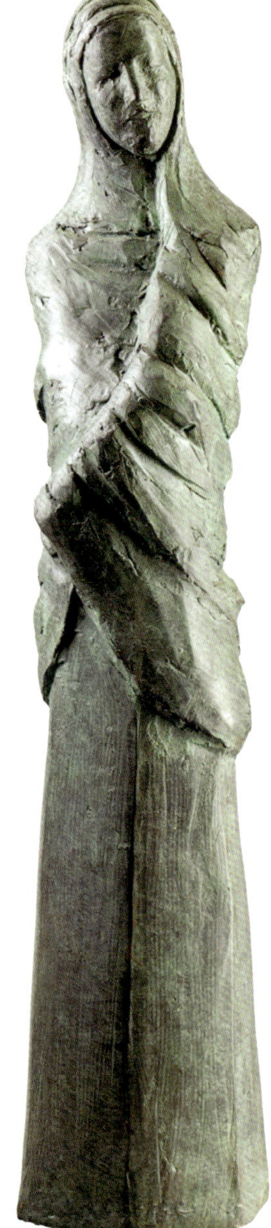

Left and Right: Briony Lawson, *Three Ages of Woman: Youth, Maternity, Old Age*, 1993. Bronze Resin

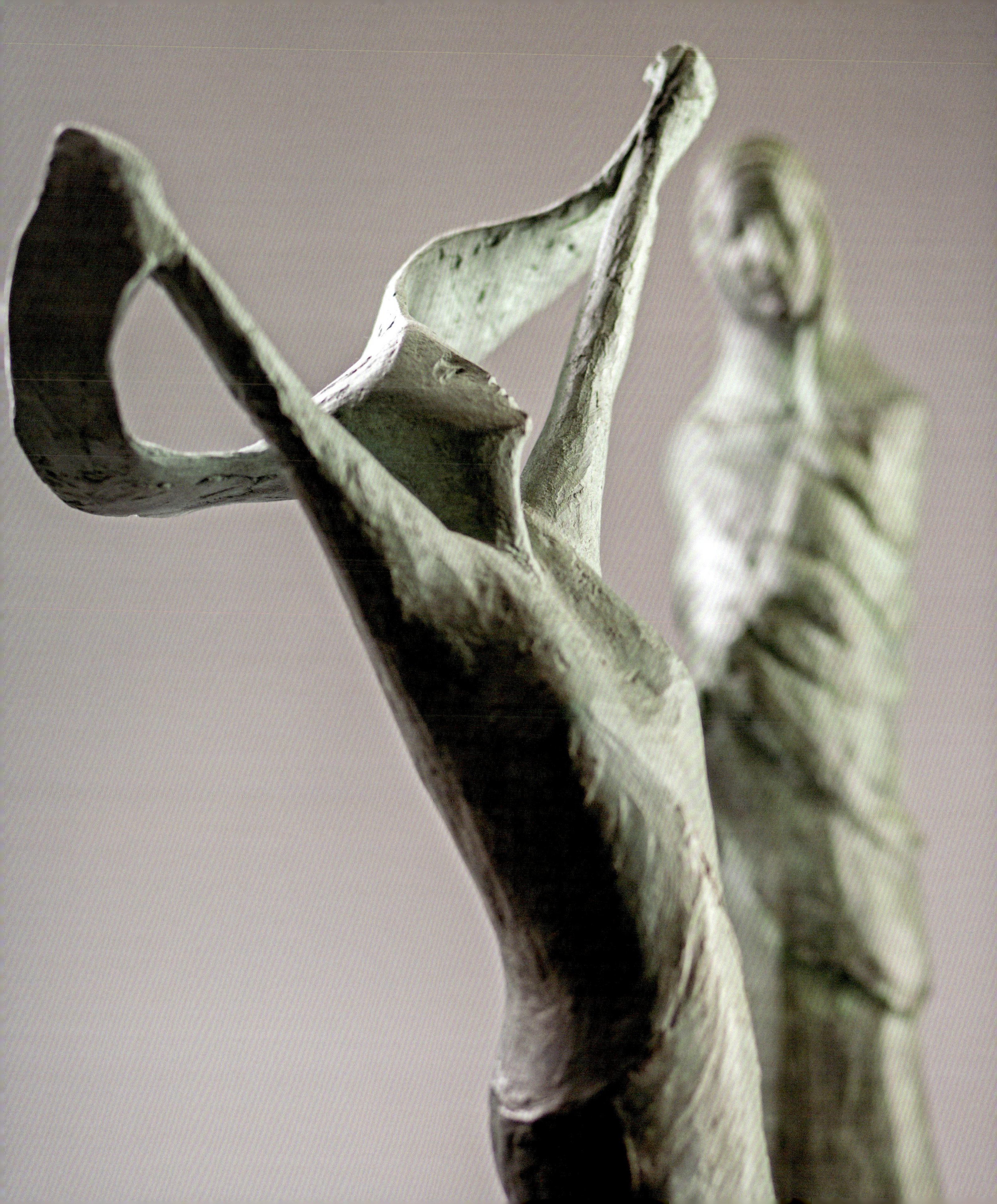

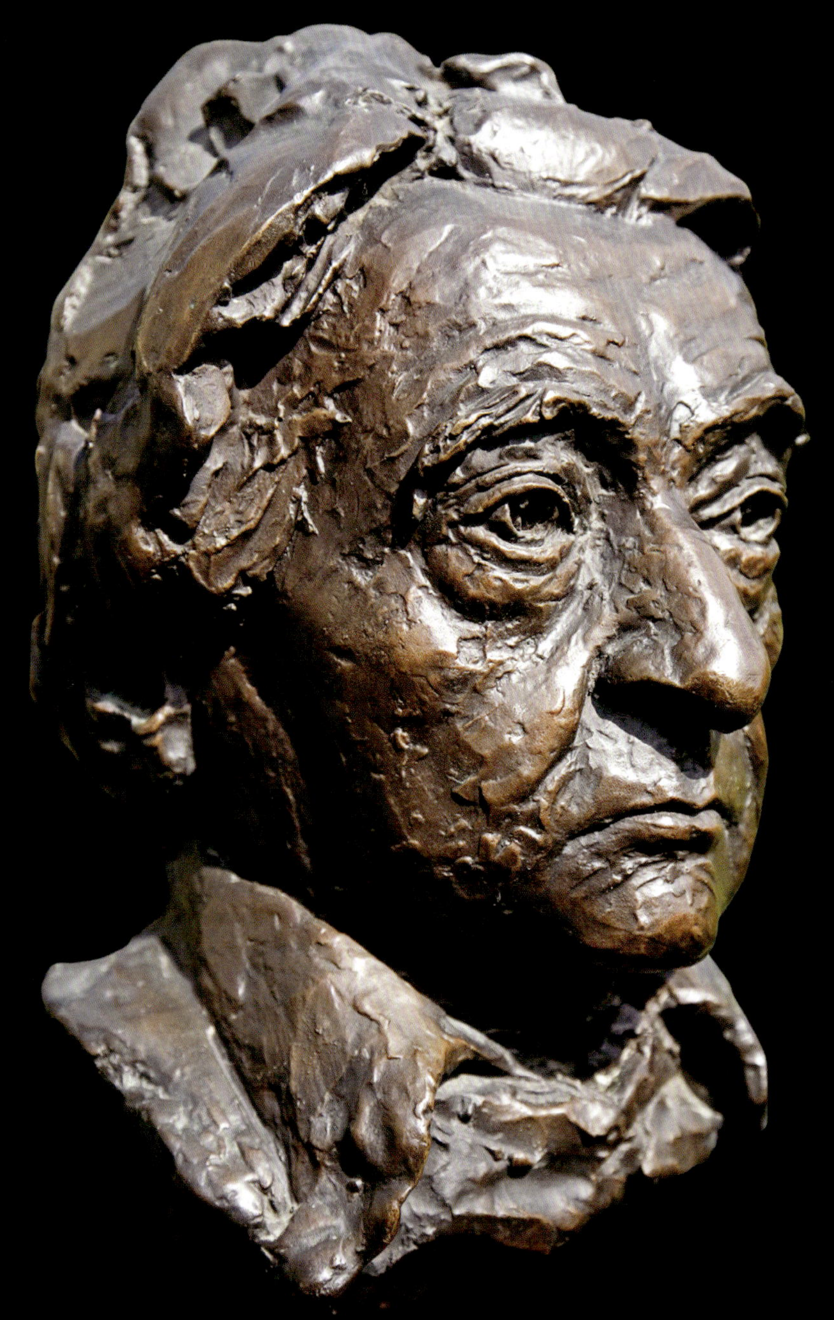

Briony Lawson,
*Portrait of her father,
Ronald Duncan,* 1980.
Bronze

Right: Briony
Lawson, *Portrait of
Andrew Lawson,* 1971.
Bronze Resin

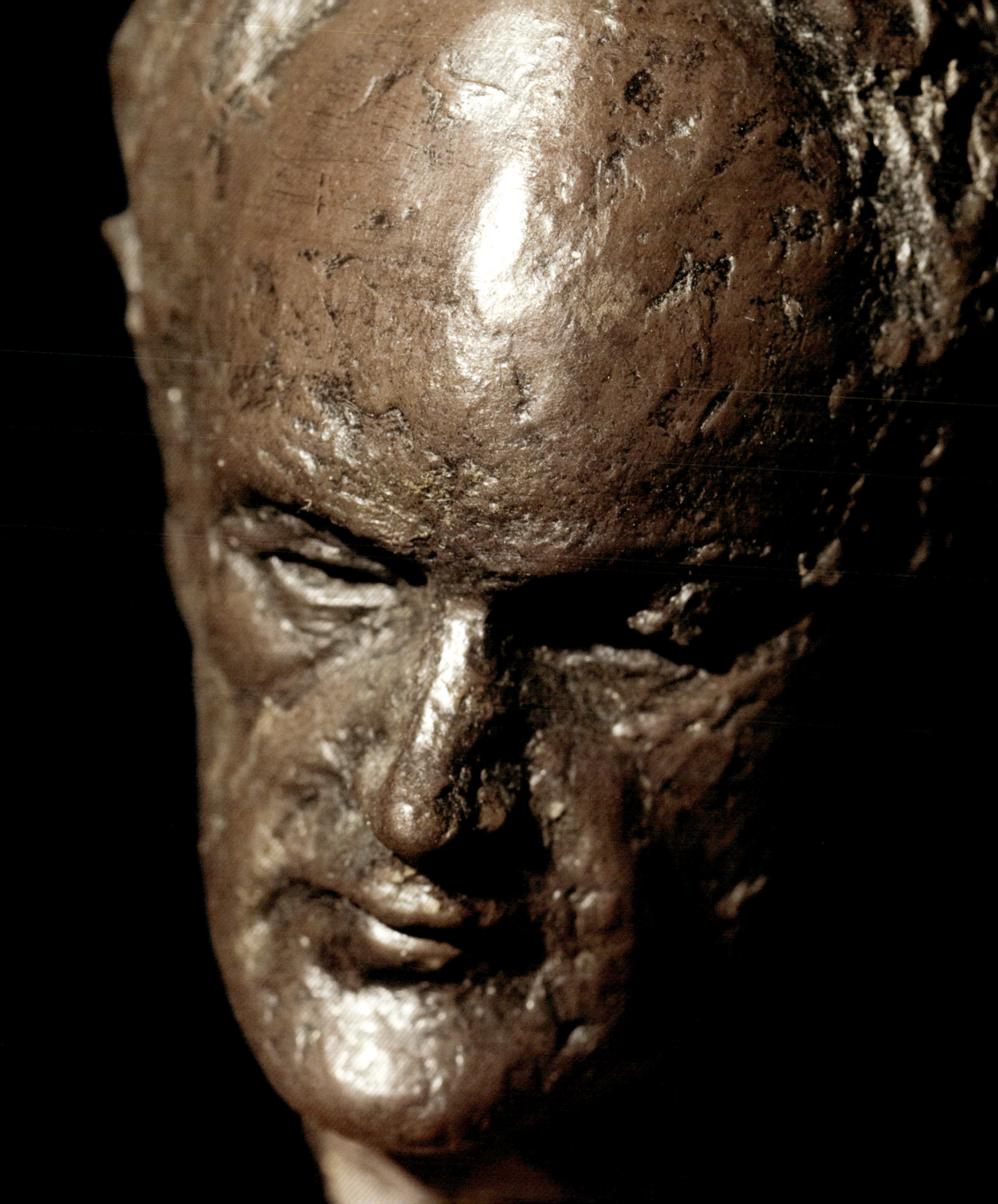

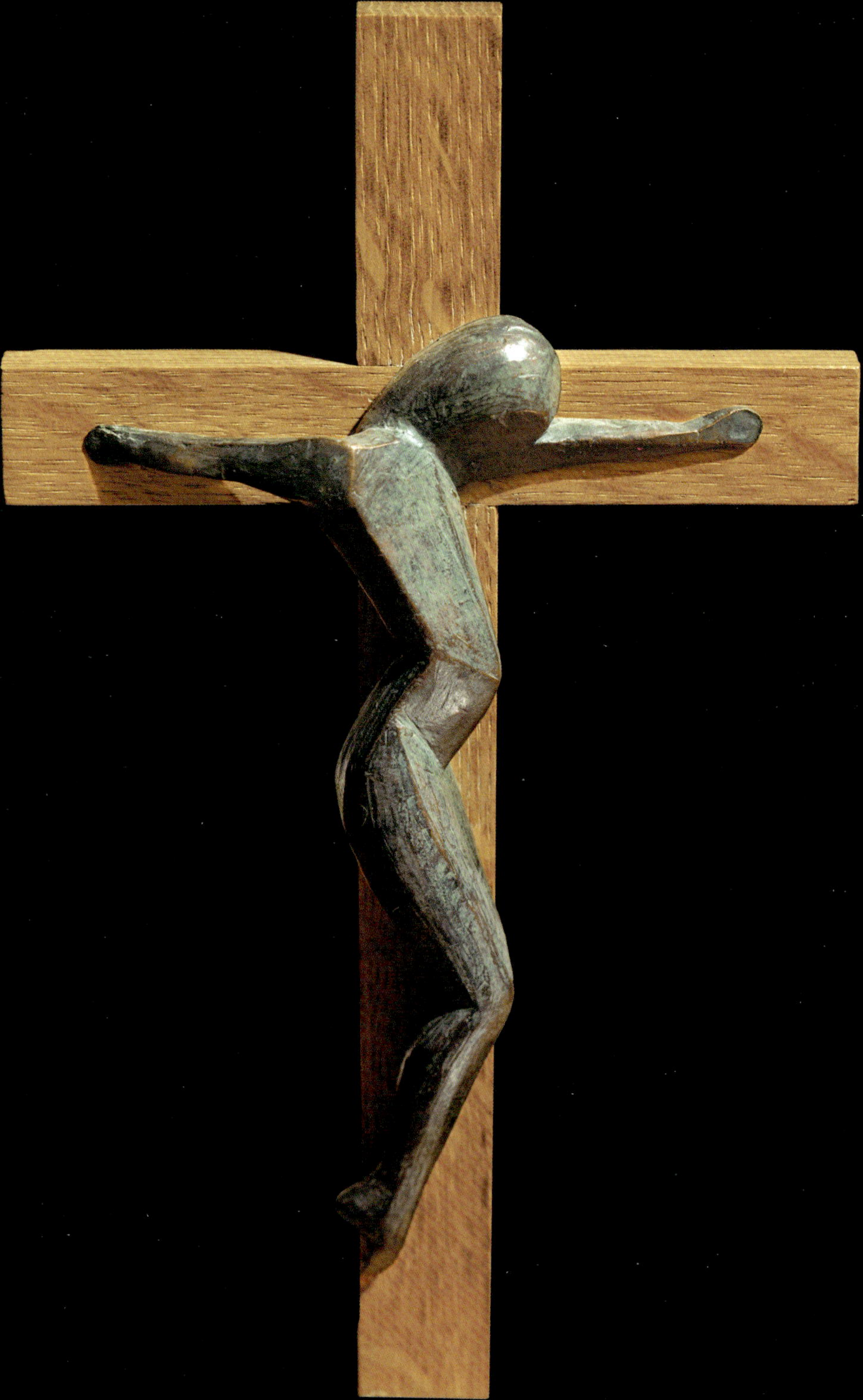

Left: Briony Lawson, *Crucifix*, 1999. Bronze

Right: Briony Lawson, *Figures for Church Wardens' Staves; Mary & Joseph*, 1994. Bronze

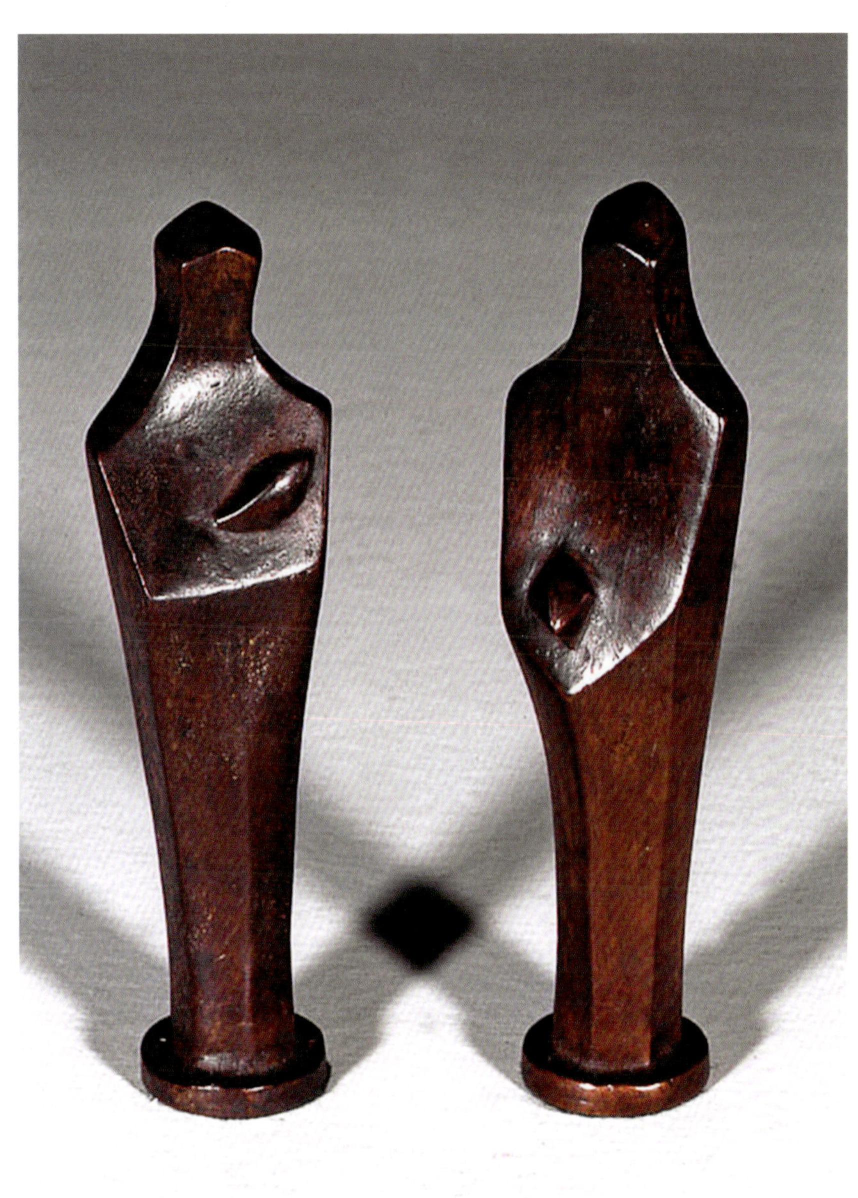

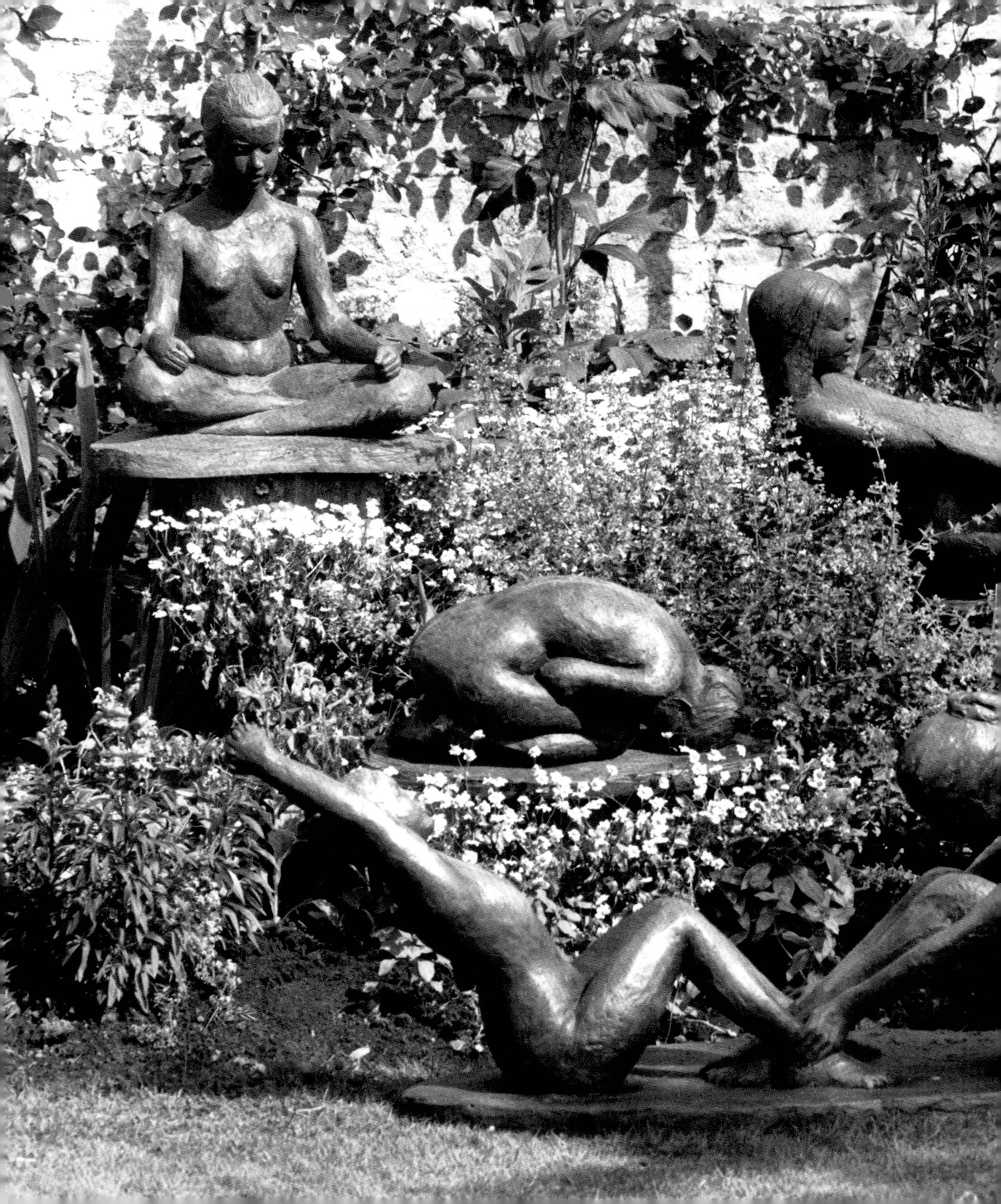

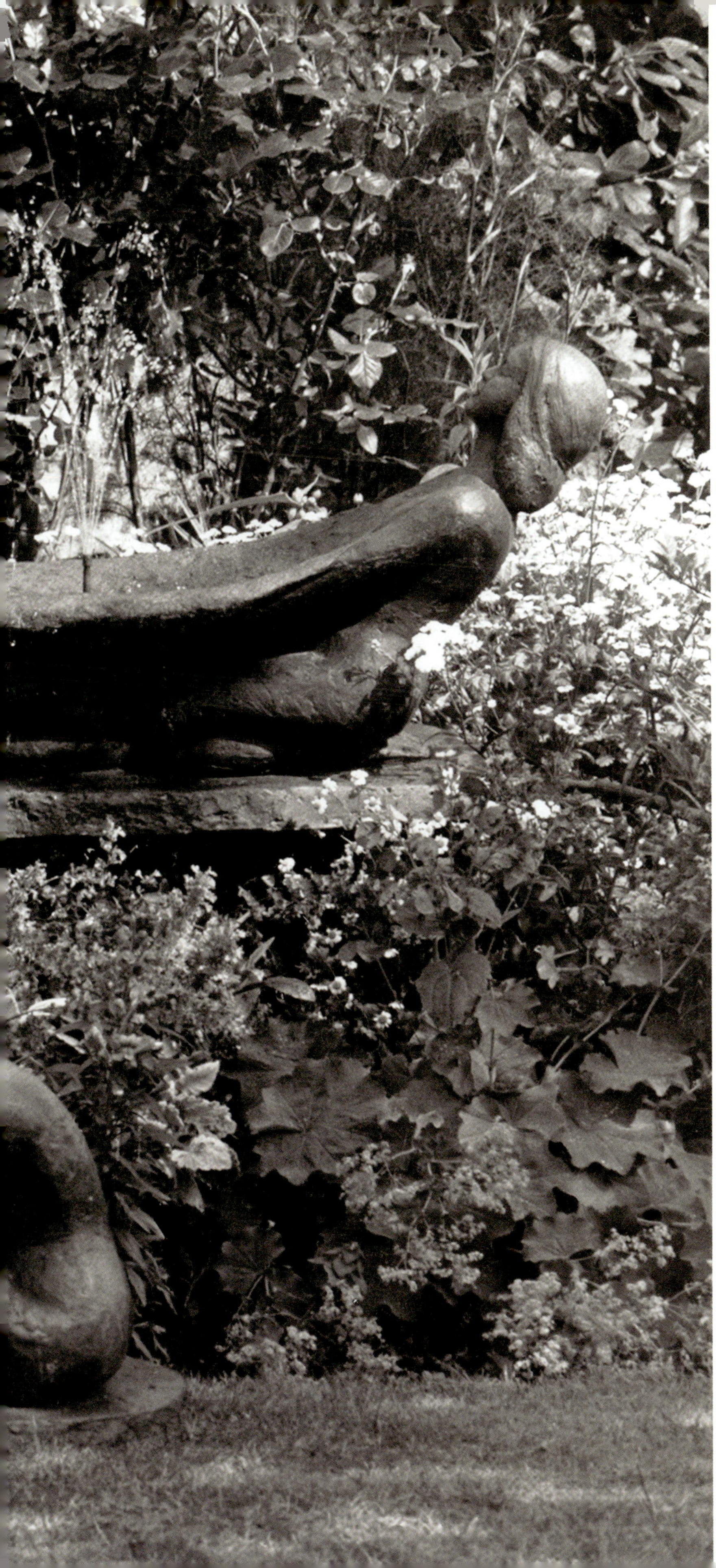

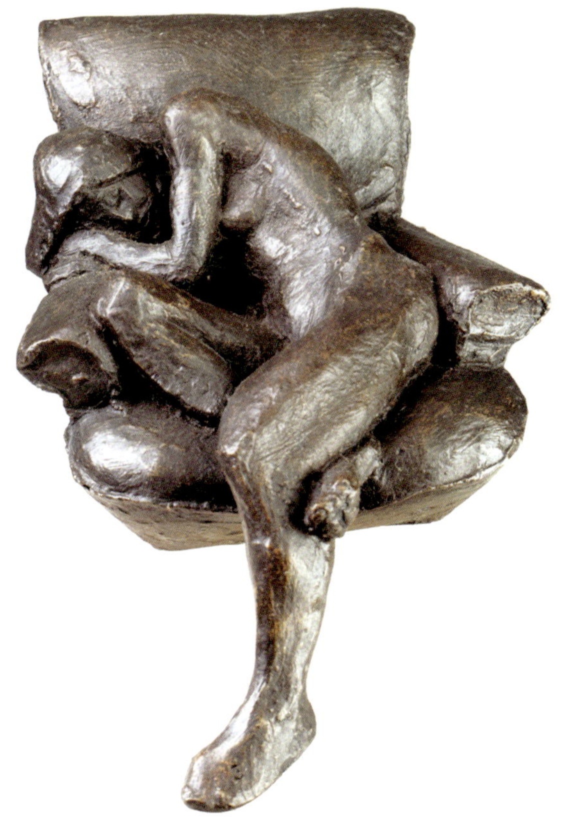

Left: Briony Lawson,
clockwise from top, *Four
Seasons*: *Autumn*, *Summer*,
Spring, *Winter*, 1983.
Bronze Resin

Above: Briony Lawson,
Seated Figure, 1973.
Bronze Resin

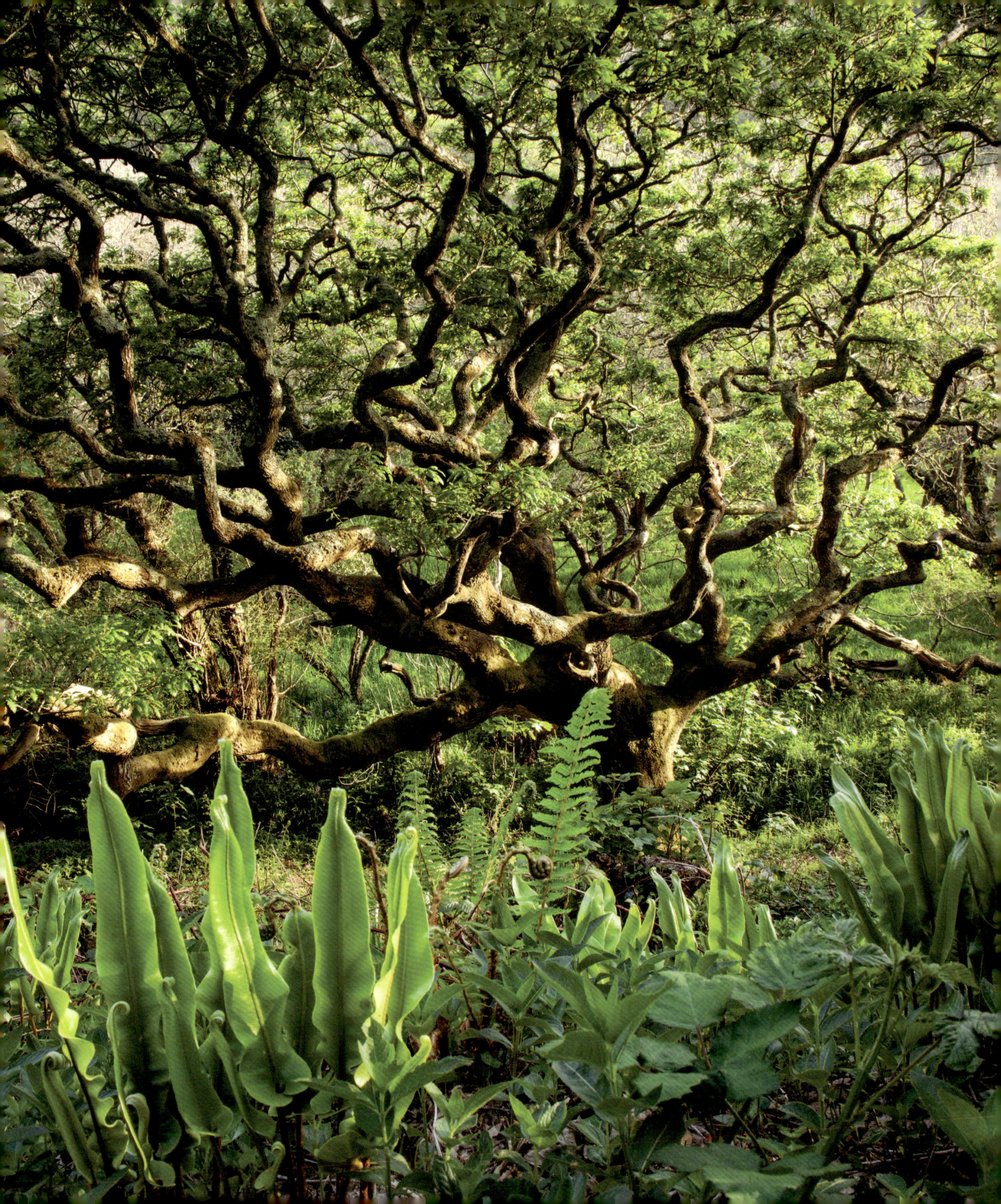

The Marsland Valley

The subjects for many of the sculptures and paintings in this book, originate from the Marsland Valley, a hidden combe that runs down to the sea on the border of North Devon and Cornwall. This is where Briony Duncan was born, where Andrew Lawson spent childhood holidays nearby, and where the family continues to occupy the mill cottage just a few hundred yards from the sea.

The valley is a nature reserve, and has a rare variety of habitats. Cut into the boulders at the sea-edge, rock pools reveal a strange pink-weeded underworld while simultaneously reflecting the sky above. On the cliff edges abundant wildflowers cling within every sheltered cranny. Tree-bare, sheep-grazed slopes give way to water-meadows, rich in wild flowers. And beyond, just inland, and protected from the wind, dense woodlands of oak and sycamore fan out through the valley's upper slopes. The harsh climate and their precarious footings on the hillside have made many of the trees grow into stunted and contorted shapes.

Threading together these different landscape elements, the Marsland stream makes its gentle and, winding passage to the sea, speeding up over rapids and resting in shallow pools.

The warm, damp micro-climate of the woodland floor creates perfect conditions for an abundance of ferns; at their best in May, when new growth unfurls above the dying fronds of the previous year.

This is the background that becomes the foreground of Briony and Andrew's work and the shared visions that have dominated their working lives. As Briony has written:

"The wild salty air of the Atlantic coast, the rocky headlands and mossy fertile valleys, give me a feeling for structure, texture and form that I have wanted, from an early age, to transform into sculpture. Whatever the medium, I always seem to turn to natural forms, whether human or plant forms, or the landscape itself."

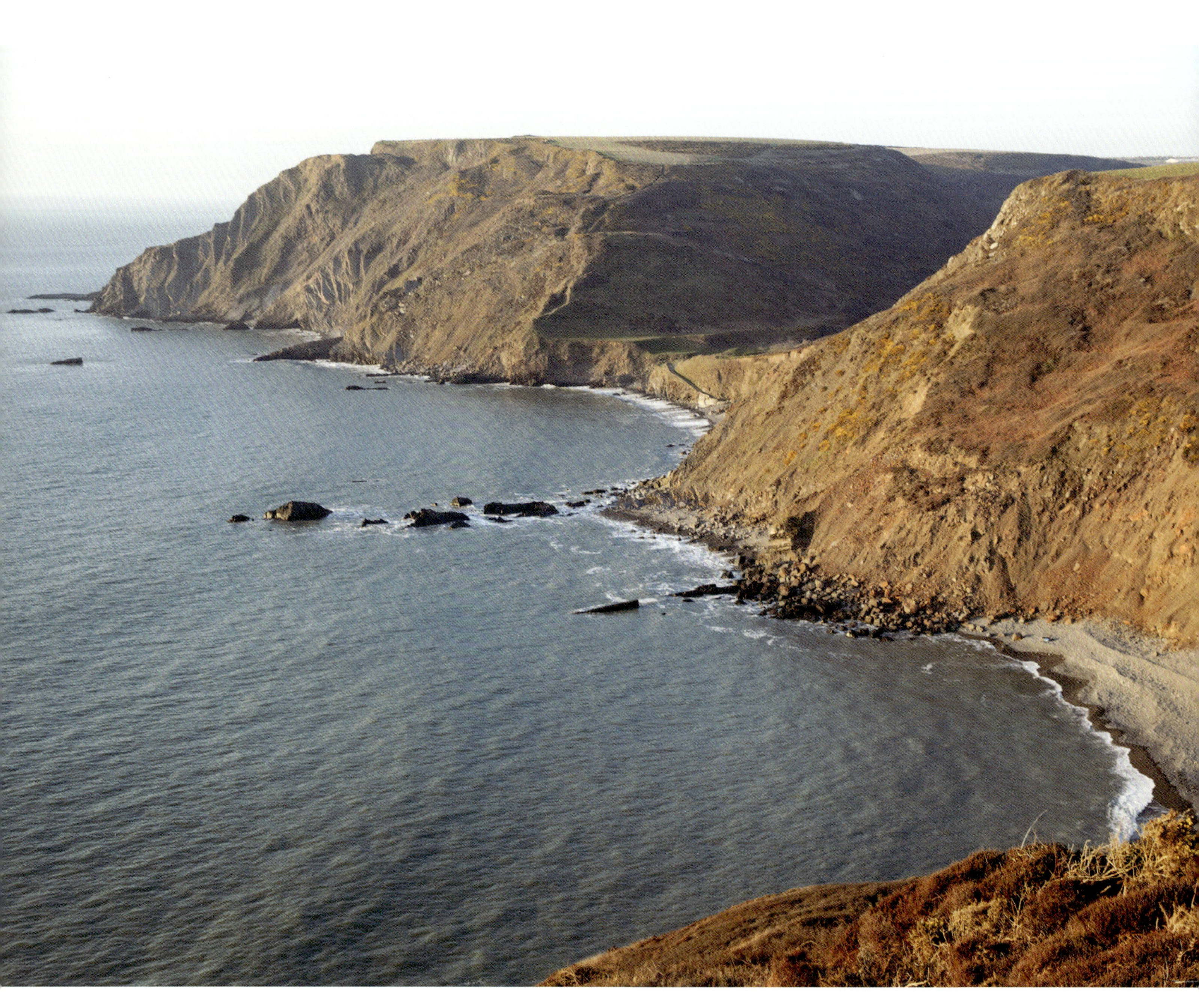

West Mill and the
Marsland valley, 2016

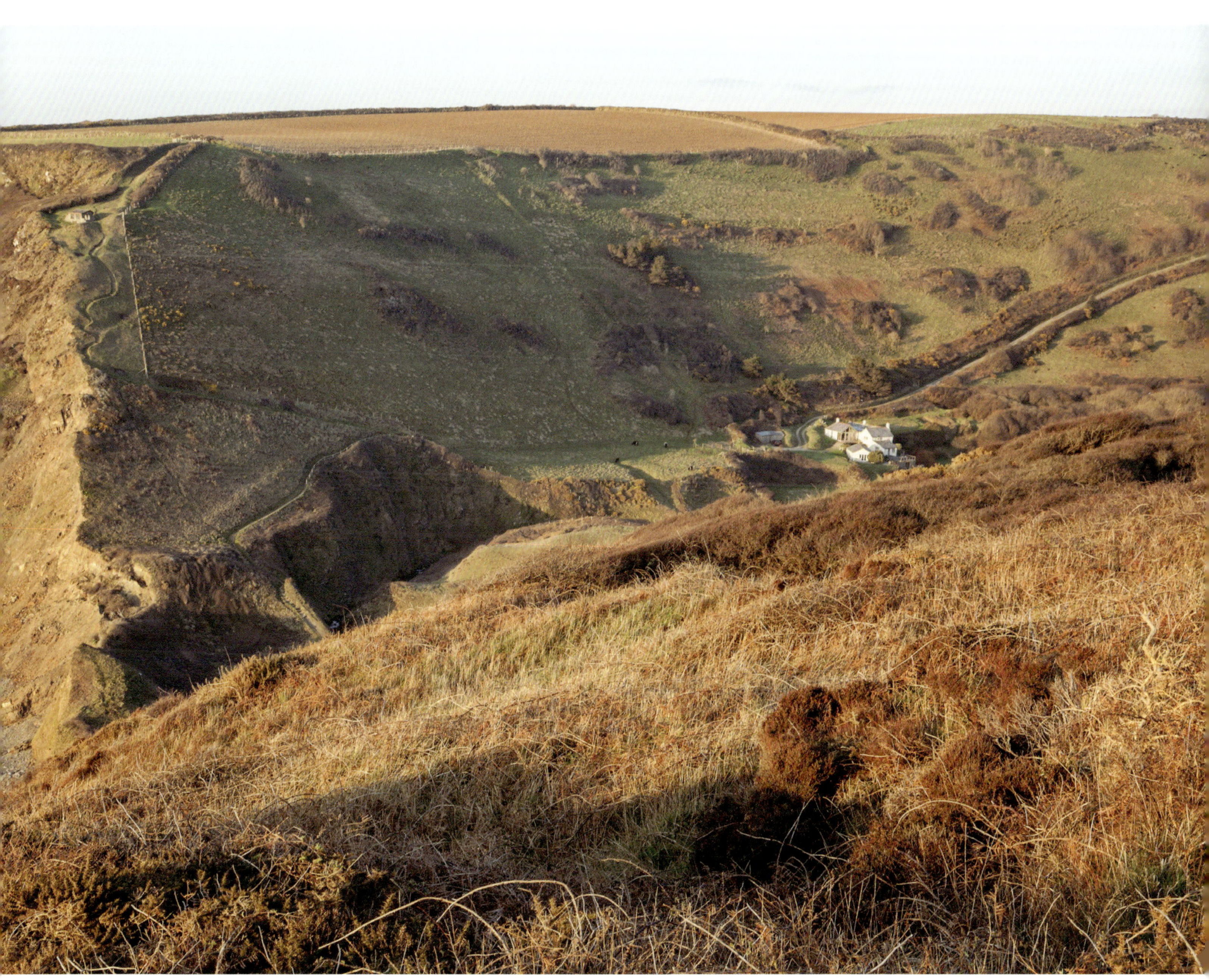

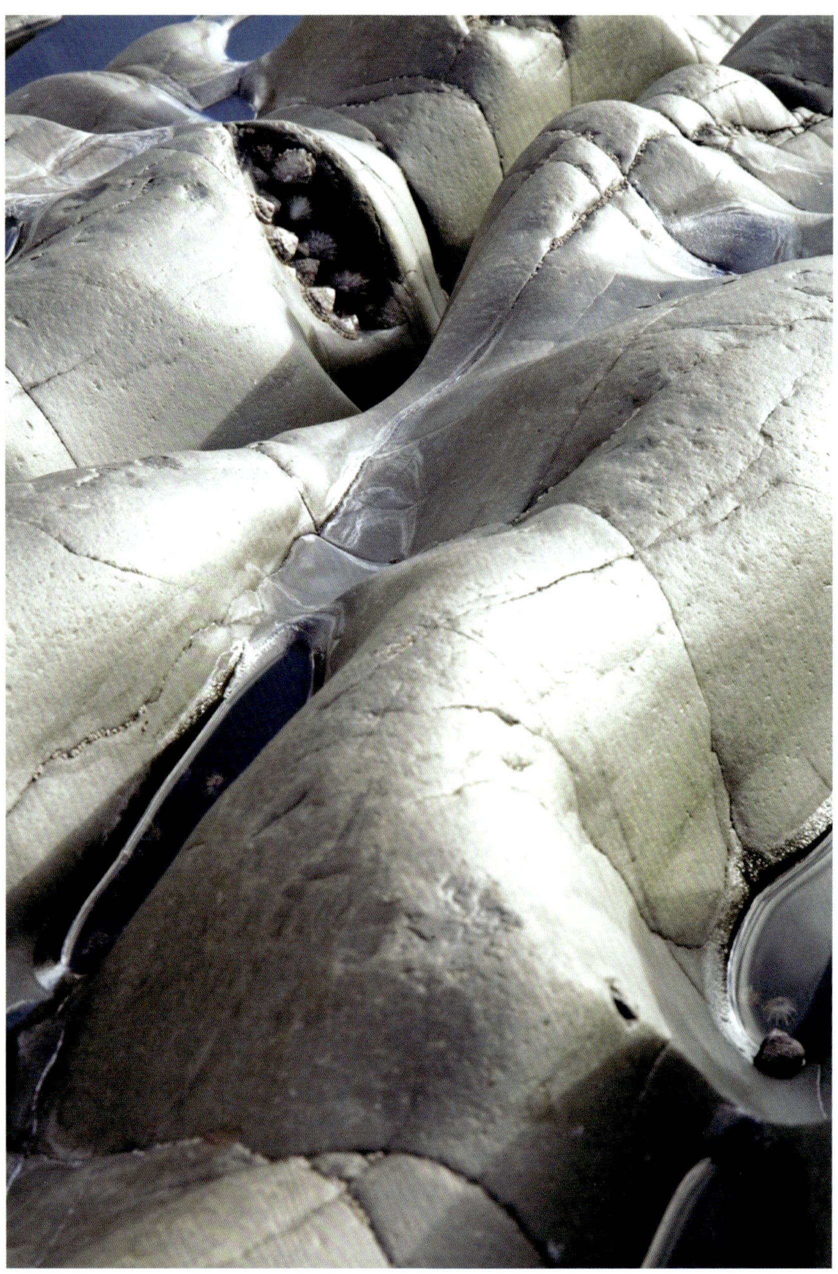

Rocks and rockpool,
Marsland, 2016

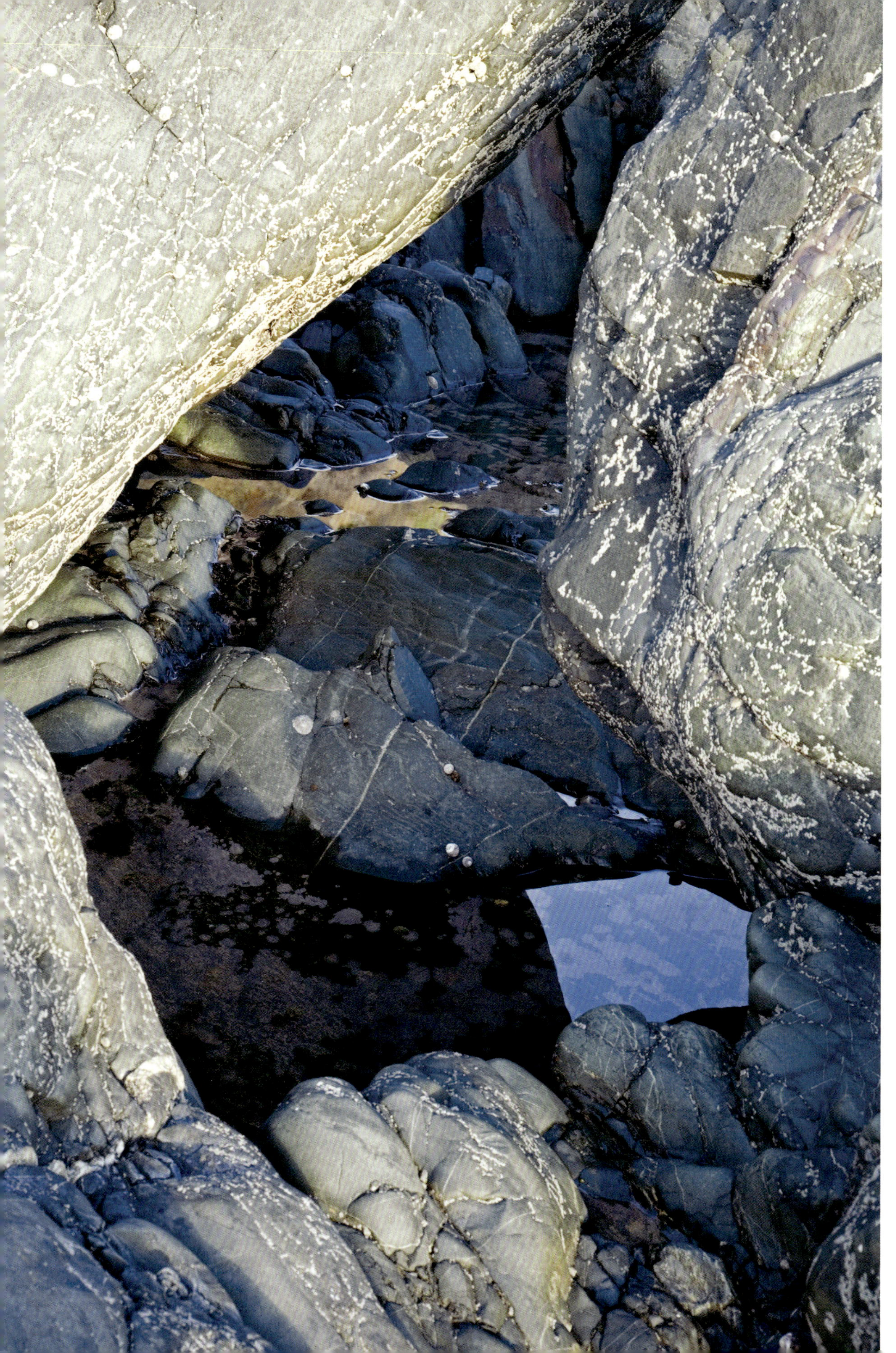

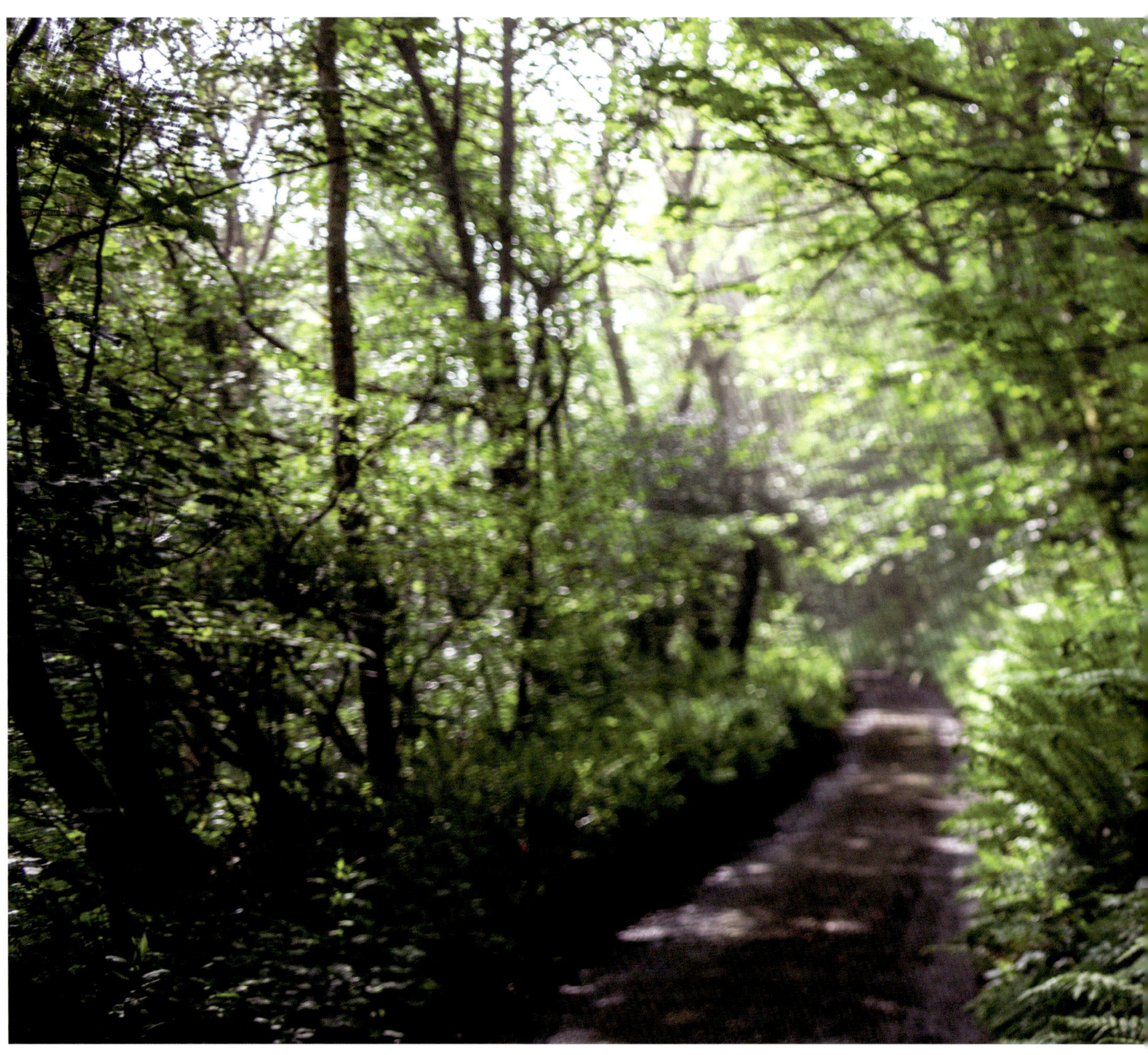

Sand Lane,
Welcombe, 2016

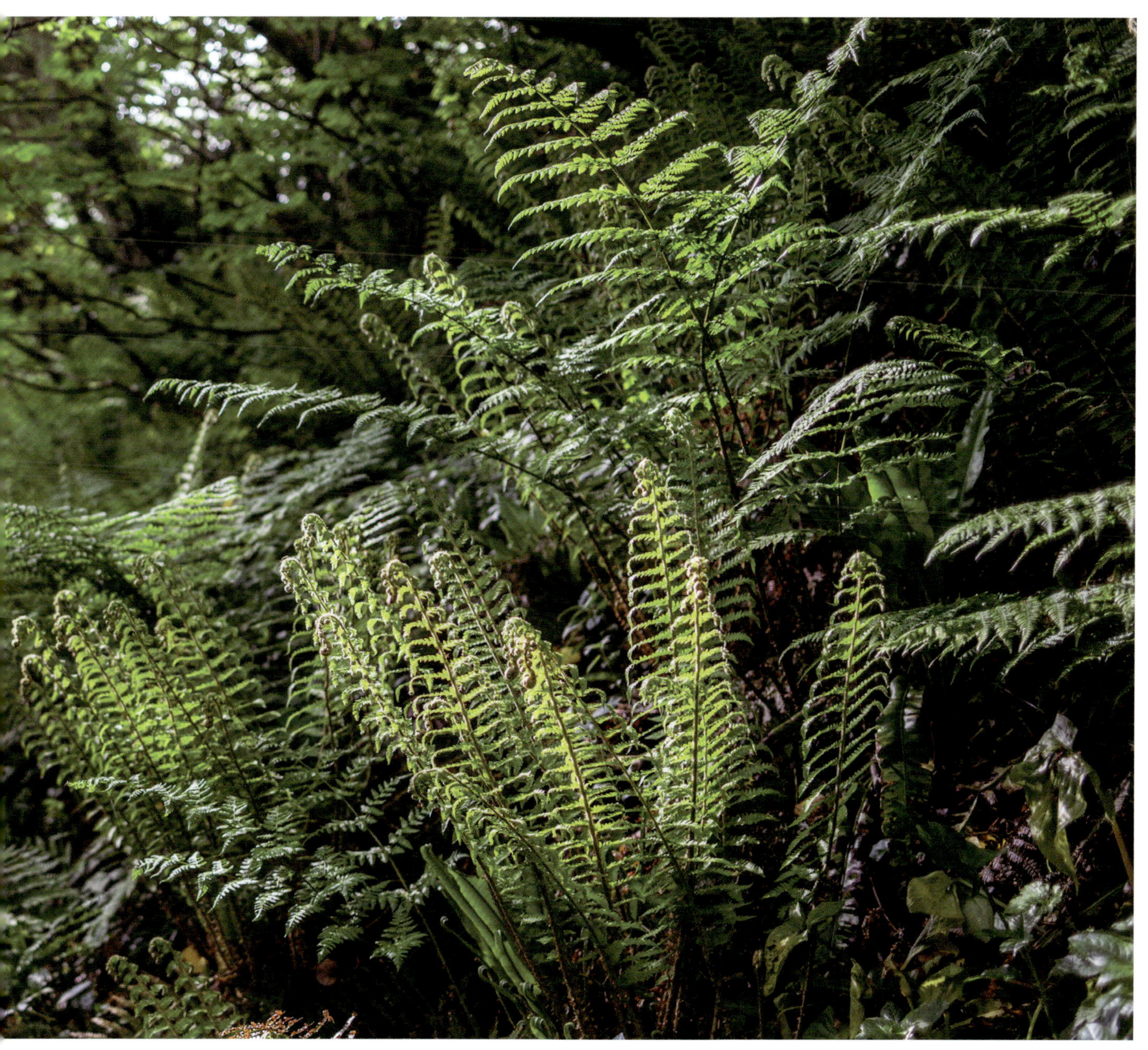

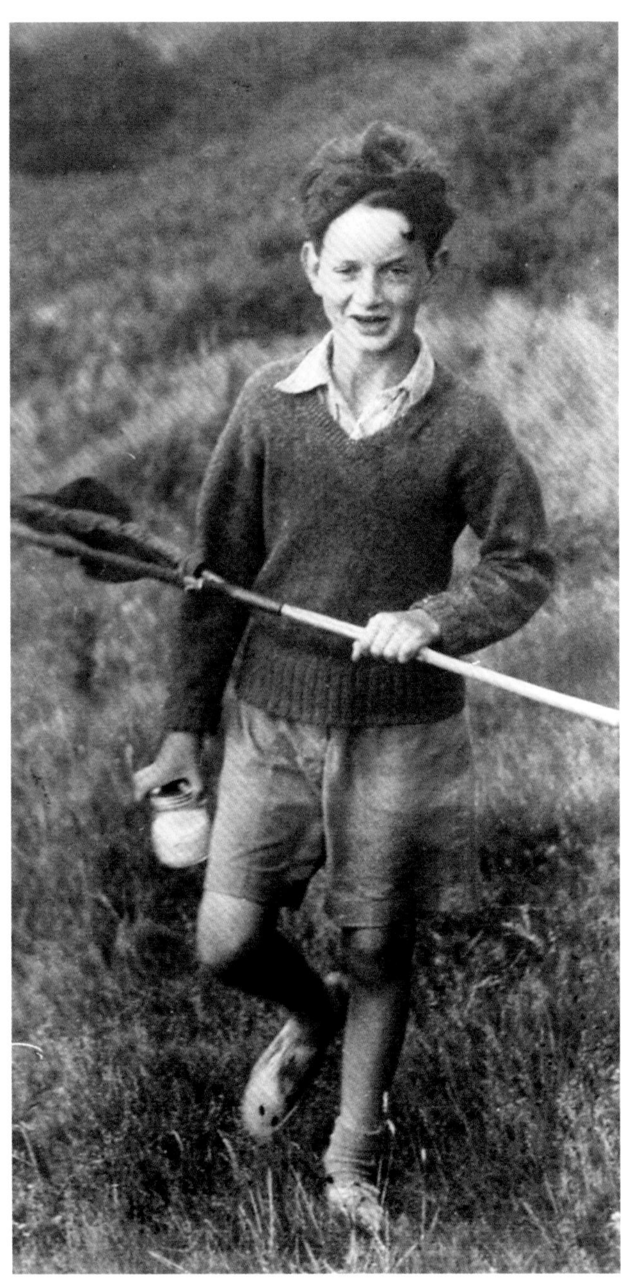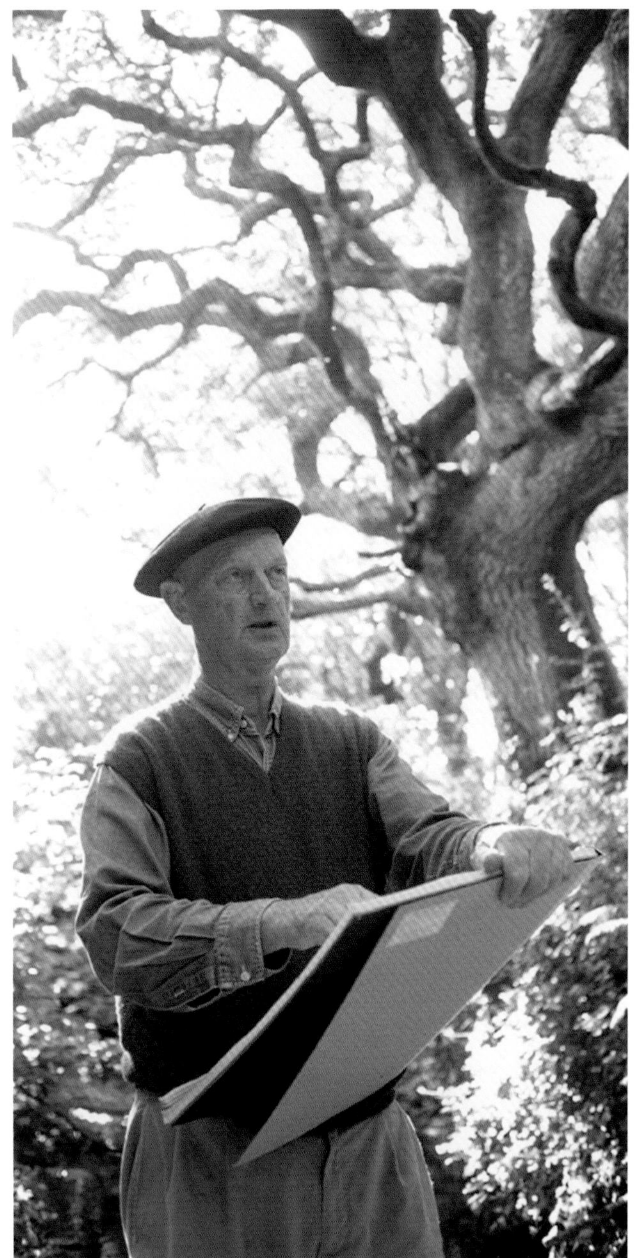

Andrew Lawson

by Tim Richardson

Known internationally as a photographer of gardens, Andrew Lawson has simultaneously – and much more quietly – pursued a career as an expressionist landscape painter. Perhaps 'career' is the wrong word, because Lawson decided even while at art school (St Martin's School of Art, London) that he was not going to follow the path of the jobbing artist, attempting to carve out a reputation by means of occasional exhibitions and gallery representation. Instead his real vocation, as a painter, would be developed privately, as an adjunct to the means by which he would earn a living – first as an art editor in publishing and latterly (from 1985) as a photographer.

This pathway ought not to suggest that Lawson has not been a 'serious' artist all along; he has simply taken a different route. In fact, in conversation it becomes apparent that it is the painting that is the point. Everything else – even the garden photography which has won him such acclaim – is incidental. Lawson is not a photographer with a sideline in painting. The opposite is true.

In common with many painters, he displays assiduous and at times obsessive traits, returning repeatedly to the same subject matter (the woods of a particular corner of Devon) and continually developing his work within self-set parameters. Yet he is also, in the best sense, a part-time artist, in that he paints only in certain environments. Lawson will make portraits or still-lifes at home in Oxfordshire, but considers that domestic milieu to be essentially his 'day-job' environment. It is North Devon which has been the wellspring of his inspiration since student days, when he first rented a secluded cottage with no water, electricity or heating, and spent blissful weeks living alone, painting and drawing in the woods. As he says: 'It's my place.' It is even more 'my place' for his wife, Briony, who was born there at the mill cottage at Marsland Mouth near Welcombe. They were

53

married in 1970 and have continued to spend substantial parts of each year at the mill.

It would be hard to imagine a more conventional middle-class world than the one into which Andrew Lawson was born, in Chobham, in Surrey. His father was an accountant who eventually became head of the profession and was knighted for his work, while his uncle had the equivalent post in the legal profession. The fifth of six children, Lawson says that his family had little practical involvement in the arts, and that he always felt that he had to find his own place in the world. As a child he was 'obsessed by drawing' and also fascinated by plants and wildlife; he was an avid butterfly collector. At Lancing College, he was able to develop an interest in graphic design by creating three-dimensional poster-constructions, somewhat reminiscent of Kurt Schwitters's collages, to advertise school plays and films (contemporaries at school included David Hare, Tim Rice and Christopher Hampton, so the quality of these productions may have been unusually high.) Lawson's schoolboy constructions bear no resemblance to his mature work as a painter, but the professional level of finish and the sheer number he completed indicate the seriousness with which he approached artistic work, even at a young age.

Art college seemed to be out of the question at this point and perhaps as a result Lawson found it difficult to tear himself away from school and its opportunities for self-expression. He spent three years at sixth form and eventually came away with no fewer than seven 'A' levels, including art and English Literature as well as the science subjects necessary for the medical degree he was to undertake at Pembroke College, Oxford. Lawson thrived in the university environment, editing the university magazine *Isis* and looking after the college undergraduate art collection which included works by Francis Bacon, John Piper and Mary Fedden. Lawson recalls hosting David Hockney as a guest speaker in 1965 taking him punting on the river and making drawings with him along with artist Patrick Procktor in his college room.

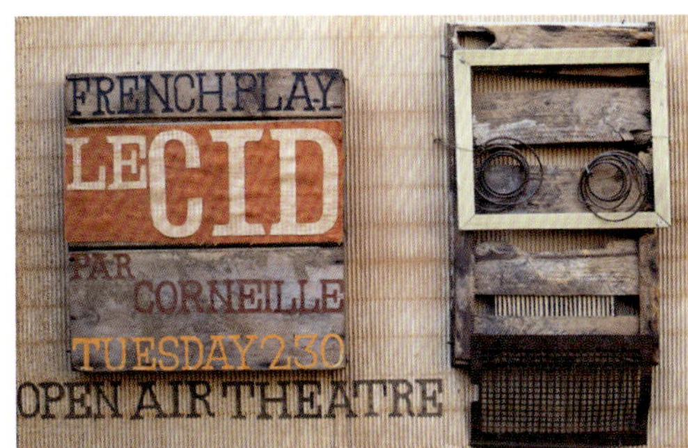
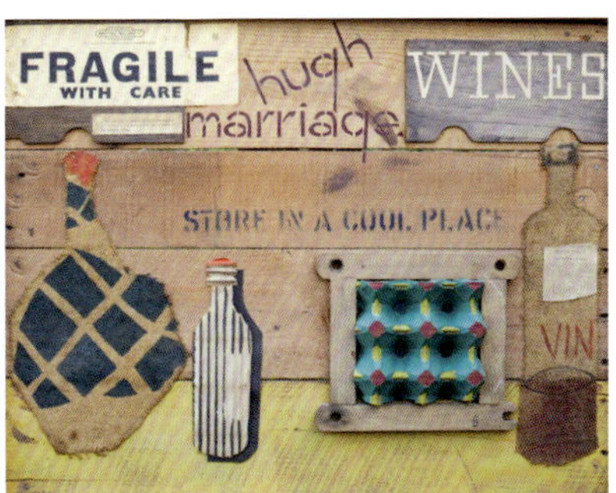

Le Cid, poster for school play, Lancing 1961. Collage. *Hugh Marriage 'Wines'*, poster for lecture, Lancing 1961. Collage.

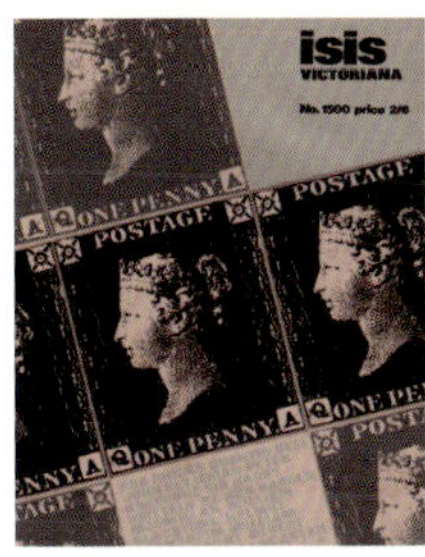
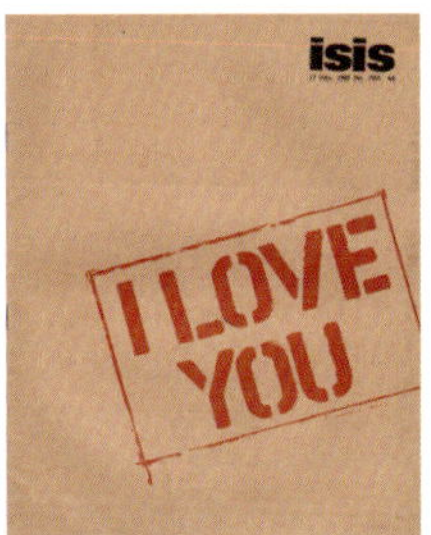
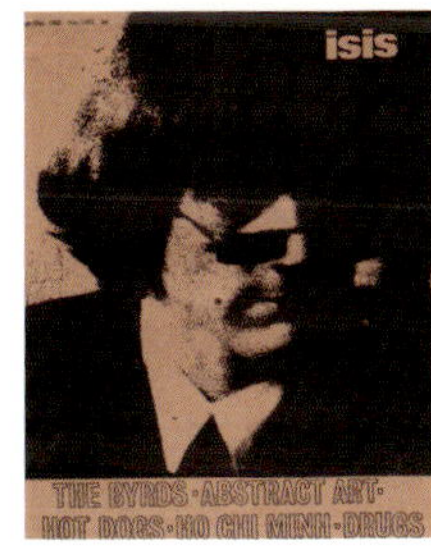
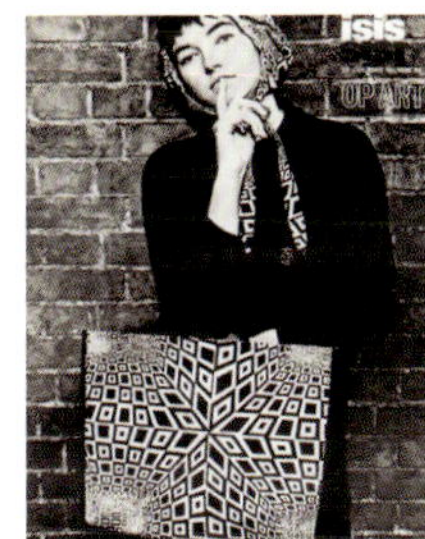

Four covers of Isis Magazine, Oxford, edited and designed by Andrew Lawson, 1965.

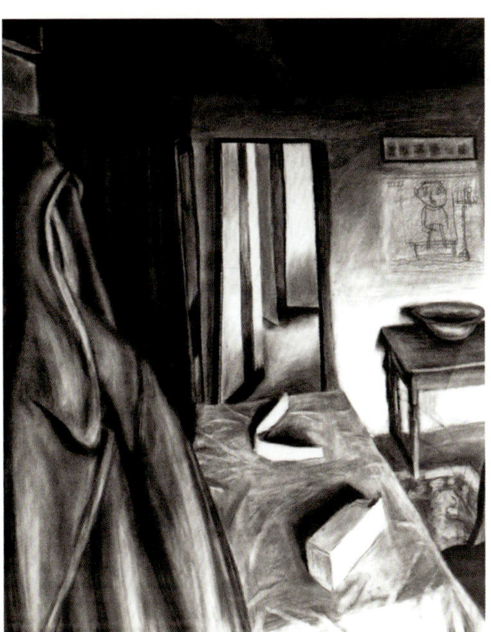
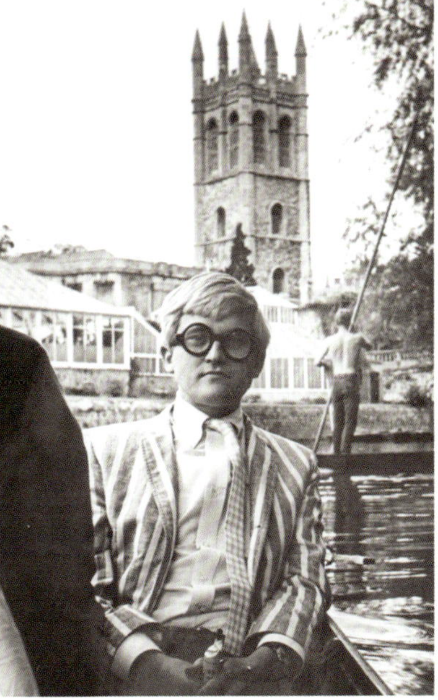

David Hockney, Magdalen College and punter, 1965. Far Left: *May Brock's Cottage, Welcombe*, 1969. Charcoal

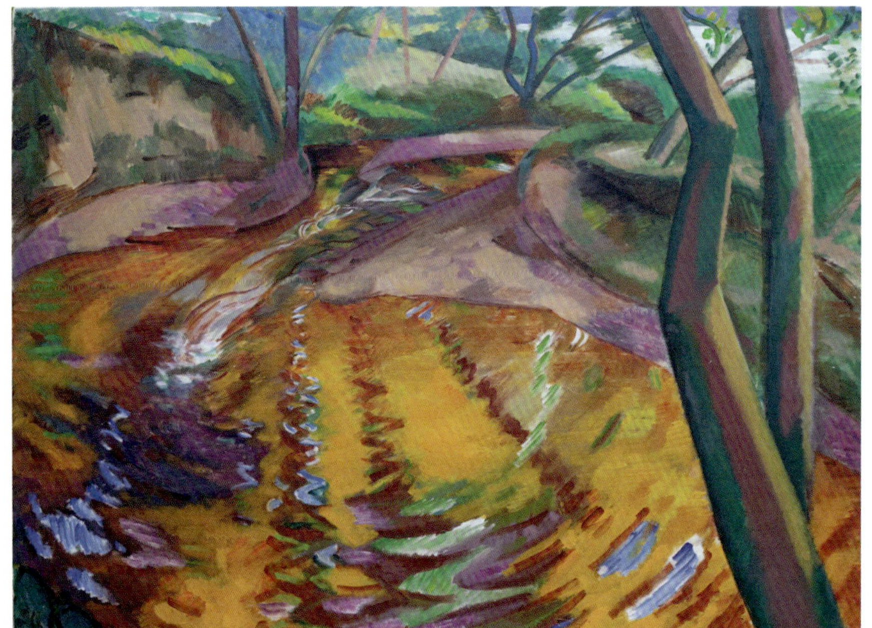

Andrew Lawson, *The Orange Pool, Marsland*, 1978. Oil on Canvas

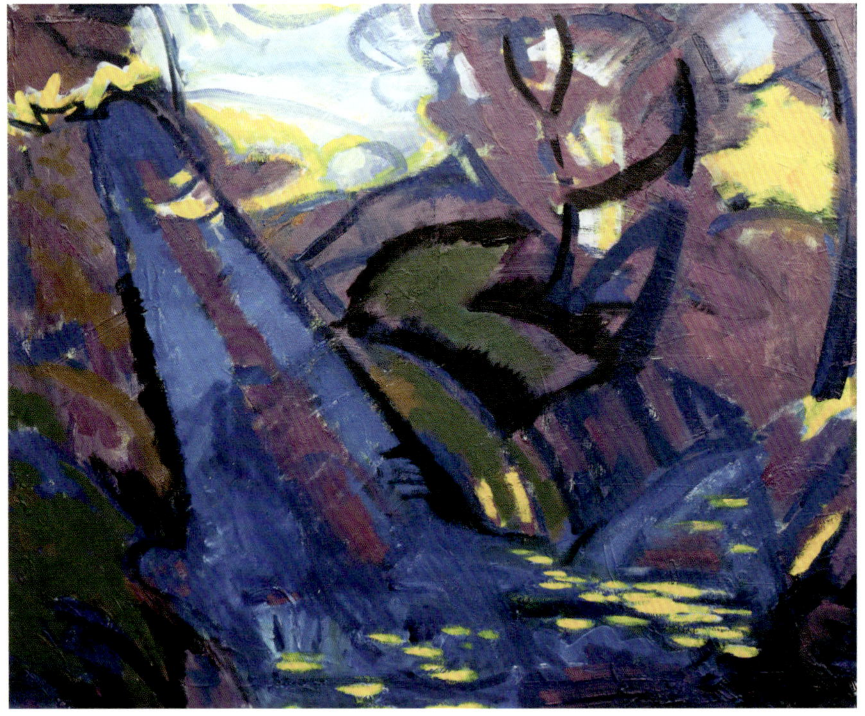

Andrew Lawson, *The Blue Roads, up and along*, 2010. Oil on Canvas

By his second term it had become clear to Lawson that he would never be a doctor. He chose to spend afternoons attending life-drawing classes at the Ruskin School of Art, but stuck out the four-year medical course and left Oxford with a BA degree. Harbouring ambitions to attend art school, Lawson felt that he would now need to pay his own way – not least because his family had been 'shocked' at his decision to abandon medicine. So he undertook work in films, at first as a runner and eventually at assistant-director level (he was assistant to Peter Brook on Tell Me Lies, 1968). He also took on freelance picture-research for the art departments of several publishing houses. It was at this time that Lawson began to rent a basic cottage in Devon in order to paint en plein air.

With a portfolio of new work – including paintings of Devon woodland – Lawson successfully applied to St Martin's, where he was to study for four years. There were tutors, such as Gillian Ayres, who were abstract painters, but Lawson gravitated towards Peter Coker, the modernist landscape painter.

Lawson's decision at this period not to pursue a career as a professional artist had nothing to do with a lack of confidence in his own ability. Asked whether he did not 'become an artist' at this point because he was worried he was not good enough, the answer is an immediate and emphatic 'No'. He explains that his feeling was that treating painting as a career would have 'sullied it'. In fact Lawson appears to relish, quietly, the idea that the work is somehow secret, or is his alone. Many artists do not like talking about their work because it is as if by naming it, it will be destroyed, or the magic will somehow dissipate. For Lawson, it is almost as if there is a feeling this will occur even if the work sees the light of day: he very rarely shows his work in public. Not a brilliant career move. But then, this was never going to be a 'career', exactly.

As for the work, certain themes have remained more or less constant, most notably subject matter gleaned from the family patch of North Devon woods. Nevertheless a key moment came in 1979 and it had nothing to do with Devon, or England. Lawson took redundancy from the publishing firm where he was an art director (Phaidon) and moved with his young family to the Pays Basque, in south-west France. This provided him with the opportunity to explore the possibilities of bright colour, as his hero Matisse and the Fauves had done seventy five years before, and not far away. Lawson describes this as a period of joyous artistic self-discovery, resulting in scores of canvases and a freeing-up in terms of colouration.

Ultimately, though, it is not the sun-drenched scenes of France that epitomise his paintings, but those of the dark, damp Devon woodlands where he is able to capture something of the throbbing, unpredictable, slightly dangerous quality of nature in the raw. There is a kind of urgent intimacy to these scenes. Lawson observes that in all his time in Devon he has nearly always gravitated towards the woods – rarely the dramatic coast and its cliffs, which are just a stone's throw away.

Having made these observations, it might be worth adding that Lawson's work does not sit comfortably within the tradition of 20th-century English landscape painting. It has none of the self-aware mythologising of Paul Nash, John Nash, Eric Ravilious or John Piper (let alone Stanley Spencer). Nor can it be placed in the Cornish tradition, since his preoccupation is not with light, but atmosphere. Lawson's work owes more to European post-Impressionism (Matisse, of course, but also Cezanne, in terms of landscape sensibility) and Expressionism (notably August Macke). He acknowledges all these influences, as well as Georges Braque in the context of composition.

The period in France had spurred an important phase of Lawson's development, especially with regard to experimentation with colour. A range of pink, purple and terracotta tones are a constant in his Devon landscape paintings, and in some instances this becomes the predominant colour theme on a canvas. Lawson says these colours are partly inspired by the rich-red Devon earth, but he also finds purples and dark indigos lurking in shadows, in ditches and in the bark of tree trunks. The vivid yellows he often deploys serve only to make these recesses seem even darker and more ambiguous.

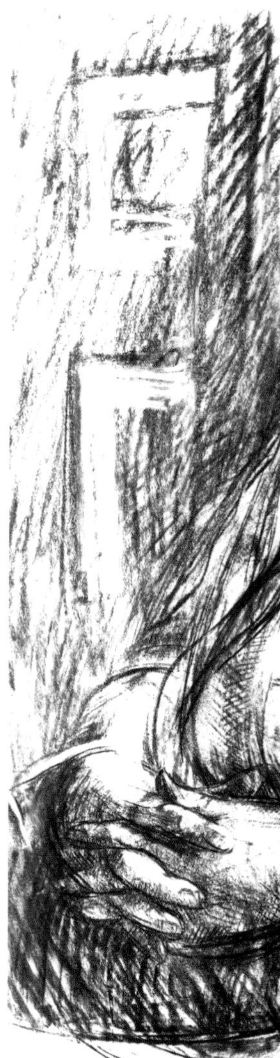

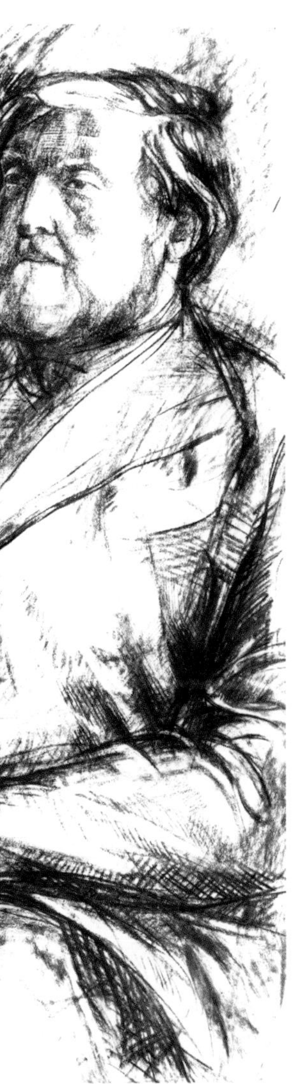

Andrew Lawson,
Portrait of The Framer,
1980. Charcoal

Lawson's paintings of woodland are always 'non-picturesque' but they are sometimes possessed of a strong compositional element – such as a line of trees which seems to meld with the wind, a long ditch or stream which bisects the scene, or most dramatically the meeting of two lanes, one plunging deeper into the valley while the other heads steeply upwards. But they are just as likely to take as their subject some apparently nondescript woodland corner, where a small mound unexpectedly rises up, or a stream seems to peter out into a bog. (Lawson quotes Cezanne's apercu that one only has to turn one's head in woodland, and there is another picture.) The focus of these scenes is usually much closer than in most landscape painting – perhaps five or six metres away. This makes them feel less like landscapes and more akin to John Ruskin's minutely observed studies of woodland moments in the Lake District. (Ruskin's focus was on plantlife, however, while Lawson's is on place-life.) These paintings are perhaps the strongest of all in terms of capturing the brimming, imminent atmosphere of semi-wilderness, teeming with a kind of life which we can keenly feel but barely understand, an energy which can perhaps only be articulated in paint, poetry and music – the harnessing of which seems peculiarly English.

There is a consistency to the work across the decades which suggests that Lawson's motivation has not been to empty the contents of his psyche across the canvas but somehow to capture something of the personality, particularity and profundity of the locale to which he has been drawn. The place is the point; the point is the place. He says his intention is 'nearly always to save the moment before it disappears' and also 'to convey what is permanent about the place'. In this context he notes the paradox of the butterfly collector. In the act of saving something of the beauty of nature, he participates in its capture and killing. The word 'fugitive' therefore springs to mind in the context of all Lawson's work. Here is a fugitive from Surrey, Oxford and the professional art world, attempting to capture in paint something of the ephemeral majesty of the natural world, moment by moment, before it runs away from us.

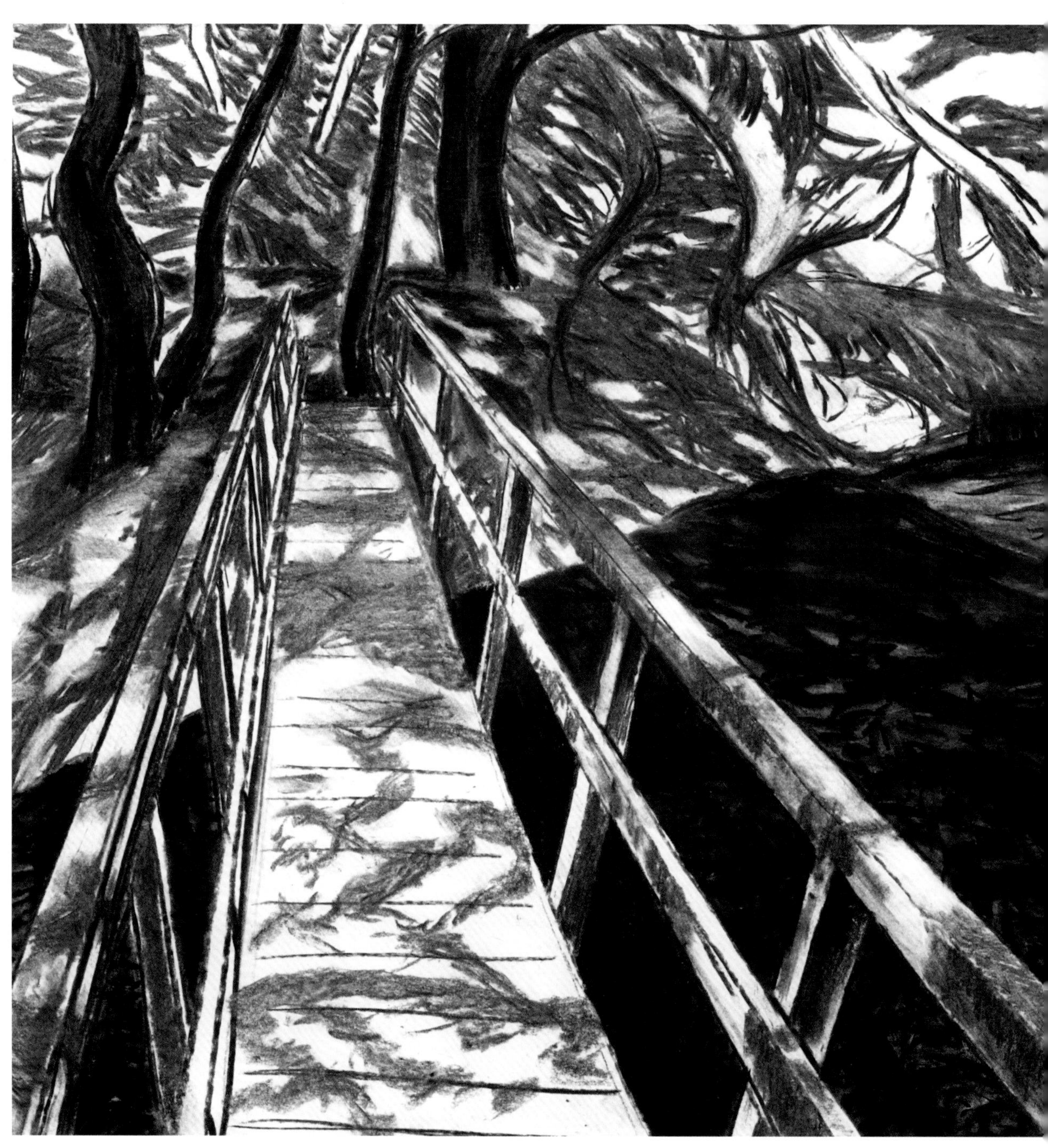

Andrew Lawson,
Travelbridge, 1980.
Charcoal

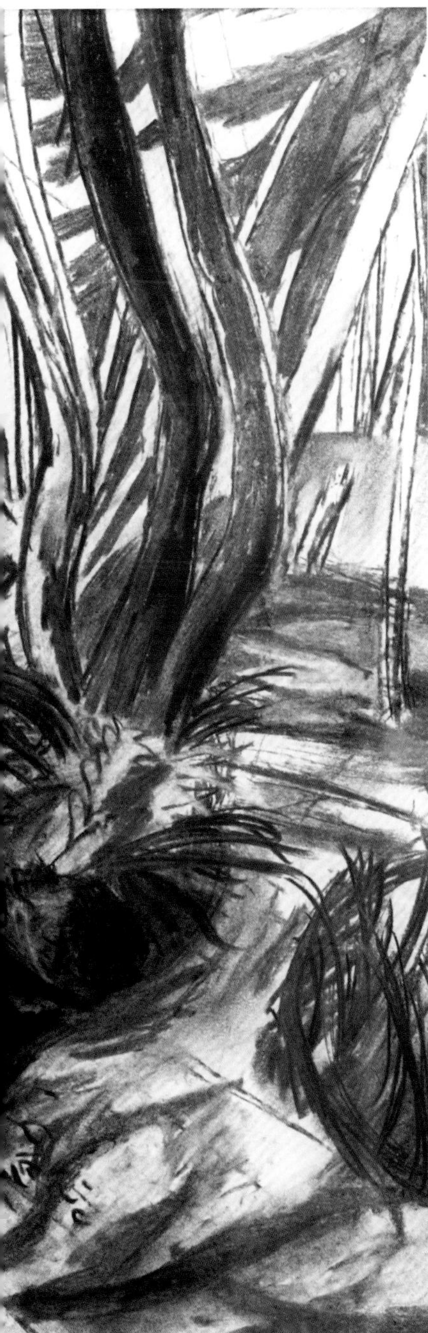

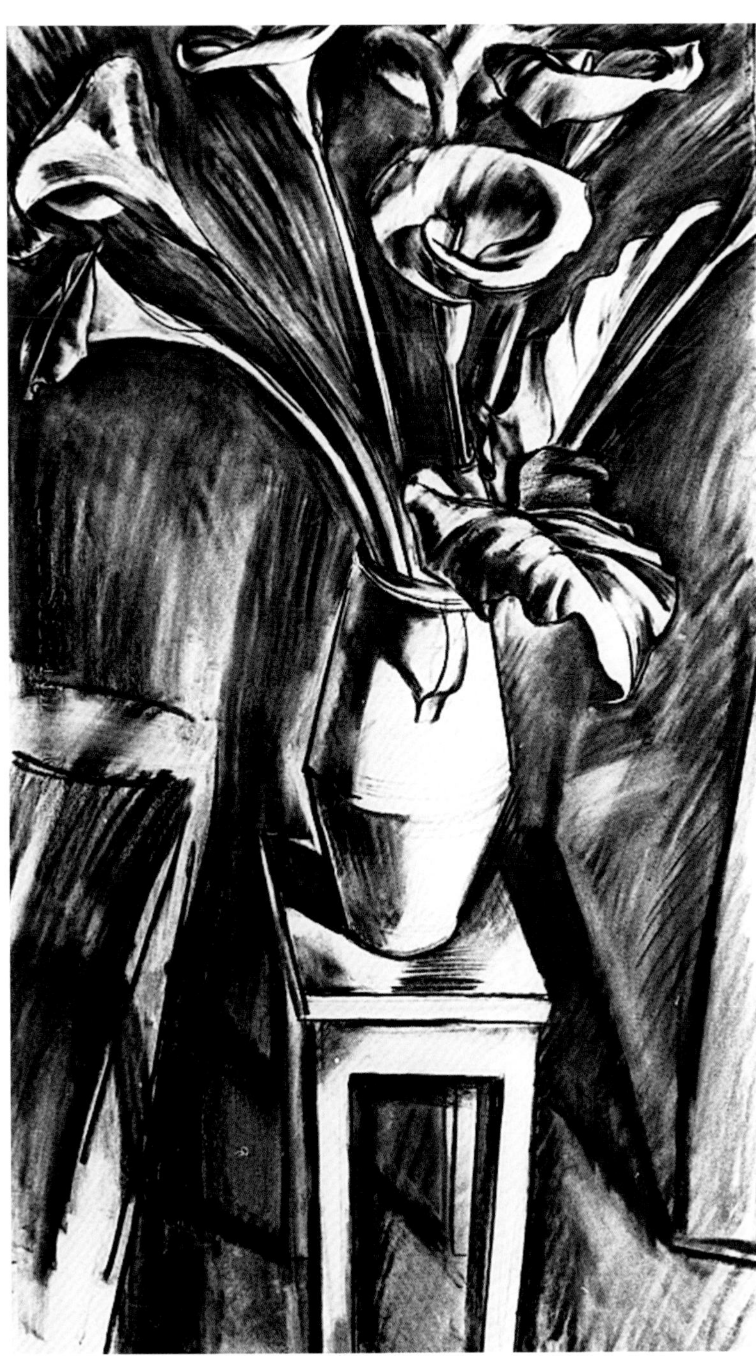

Andrew Lawson,
*Zantedeschia (Arum
Lilies) at Ostabat*, 1979.
Charcoal

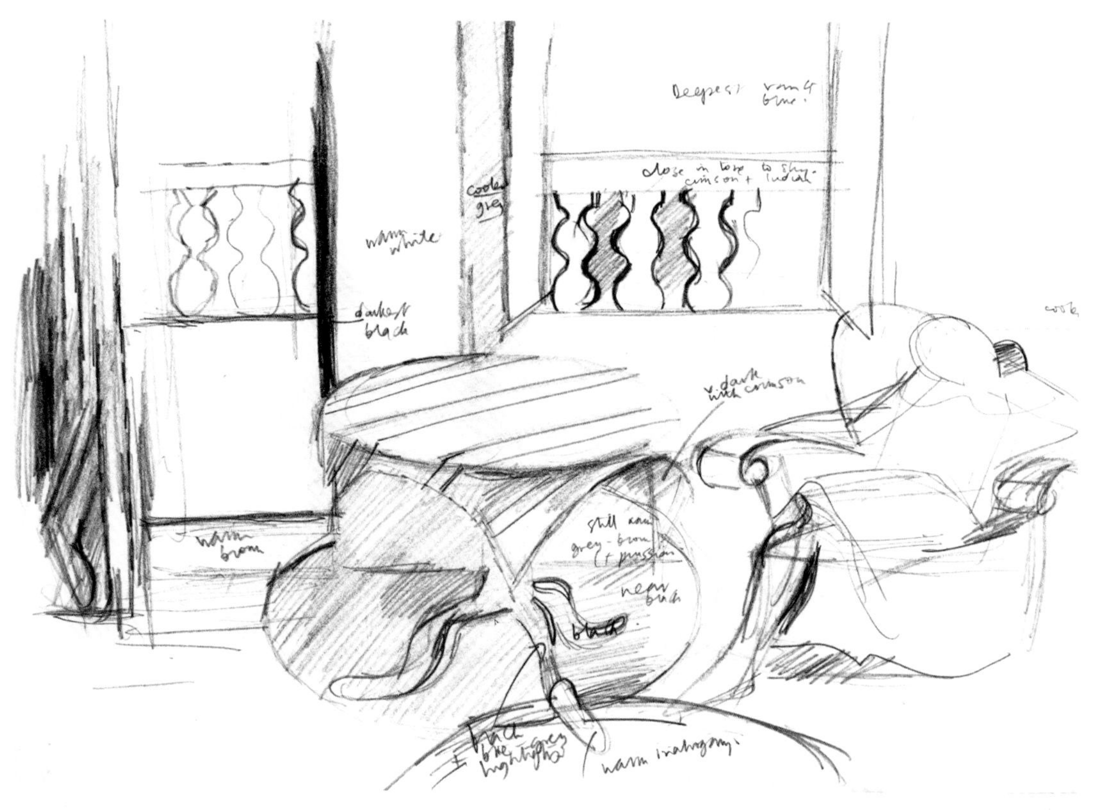

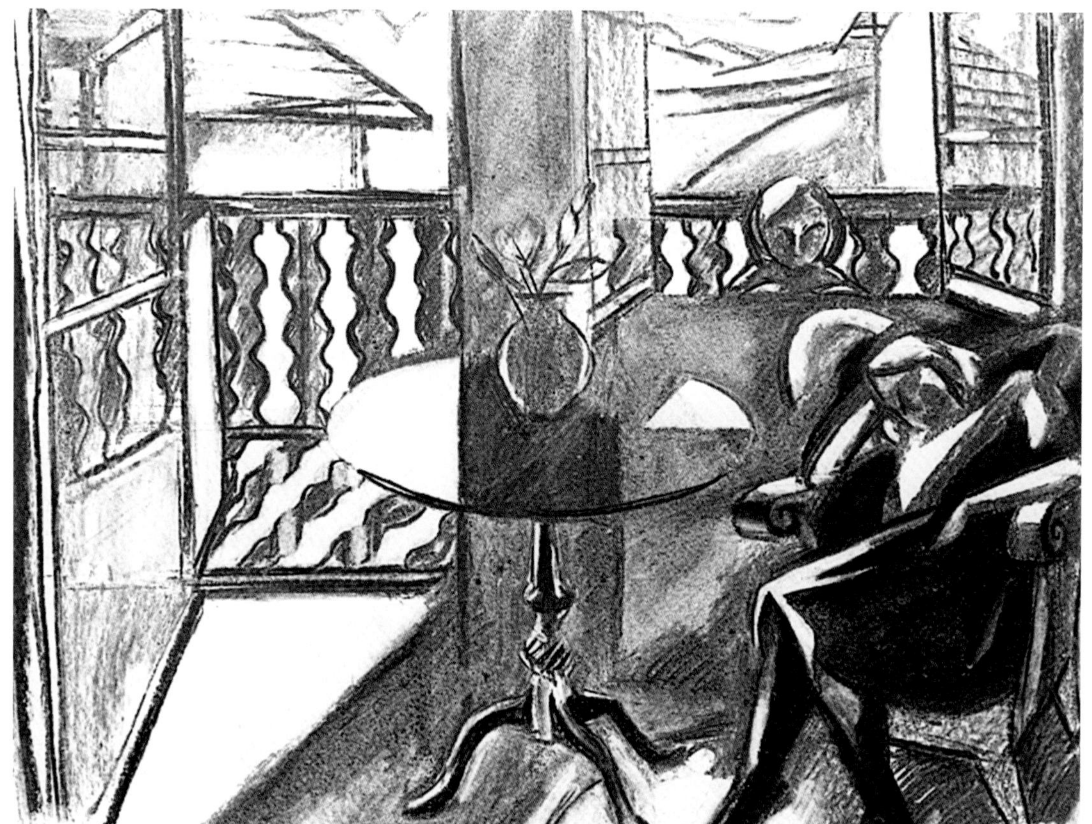

Right: Andrew Lawson, *The Balcony, Ostabat*, 1979. Oil on Canvas

Left, Above and Below: Andrew Lawson, *Two studies for the painting, The Balcony*, 1979. Pencil (top), Charcoal (below)

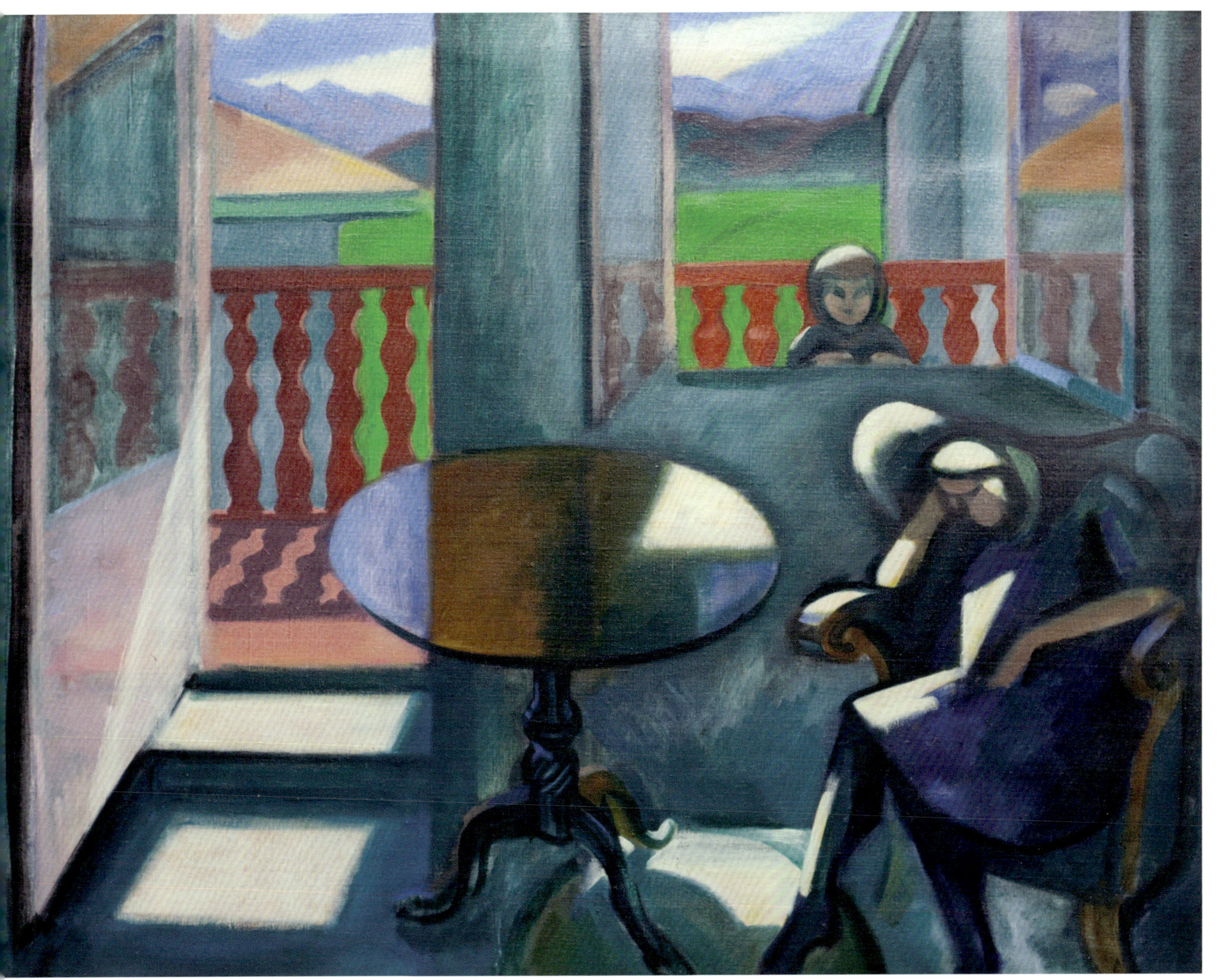

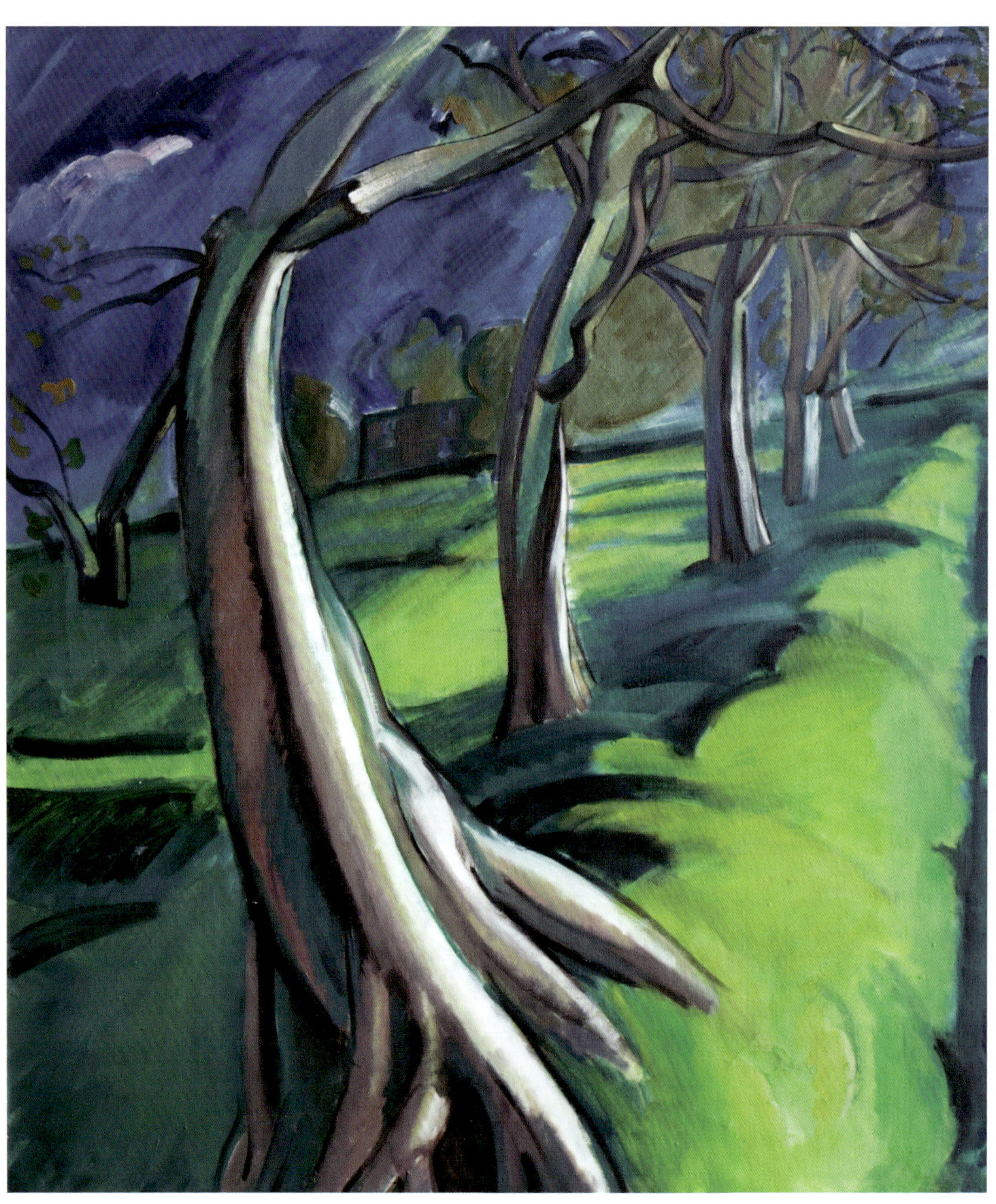

Andrew Lawson,
The Sycamore Bank with
May Brock's Cottage,
1978. Oil on Canvas

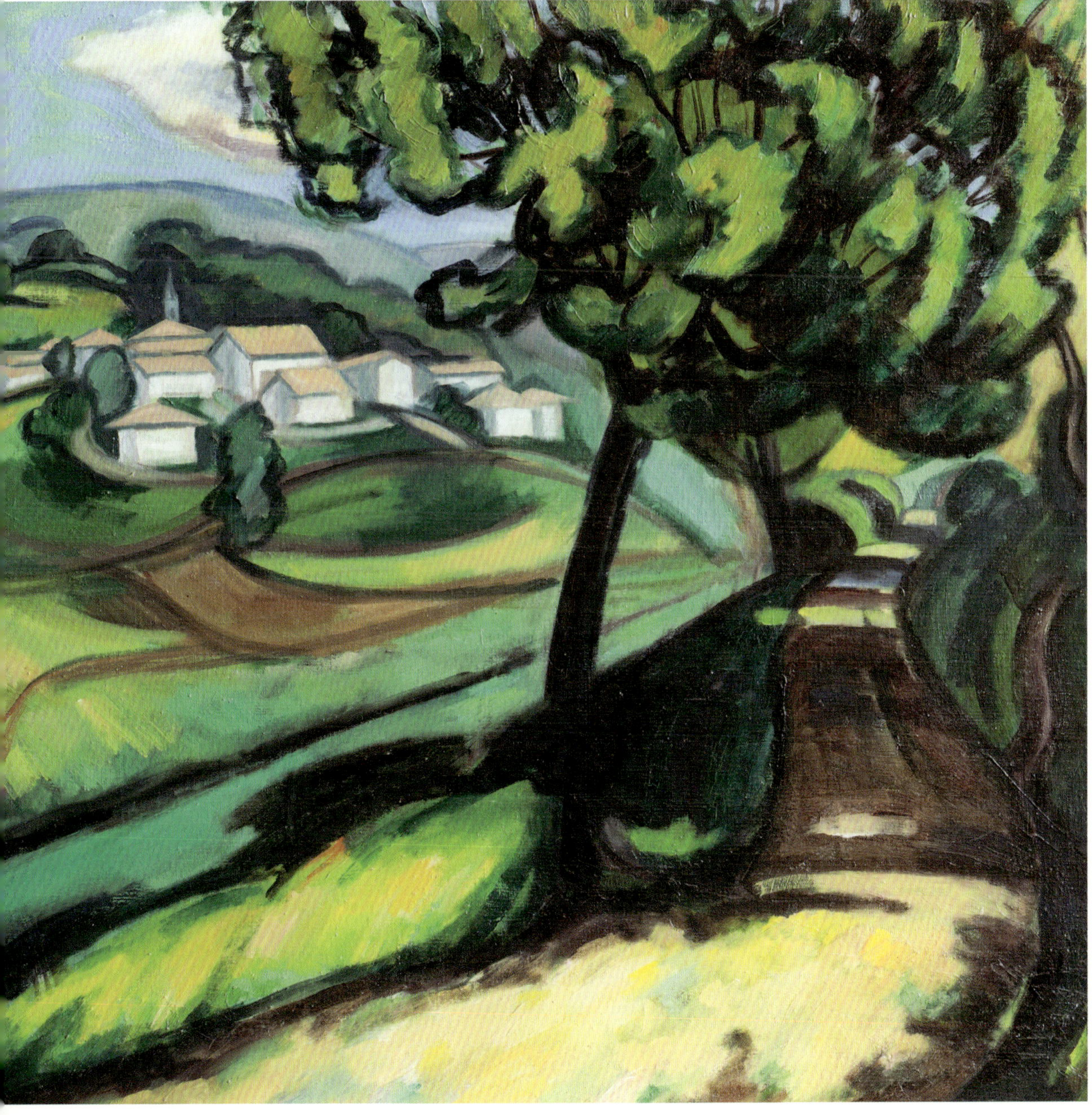

Andrew Lawson, *The Path to Compostela, Ostabat*, 1979. Oil on Canvas

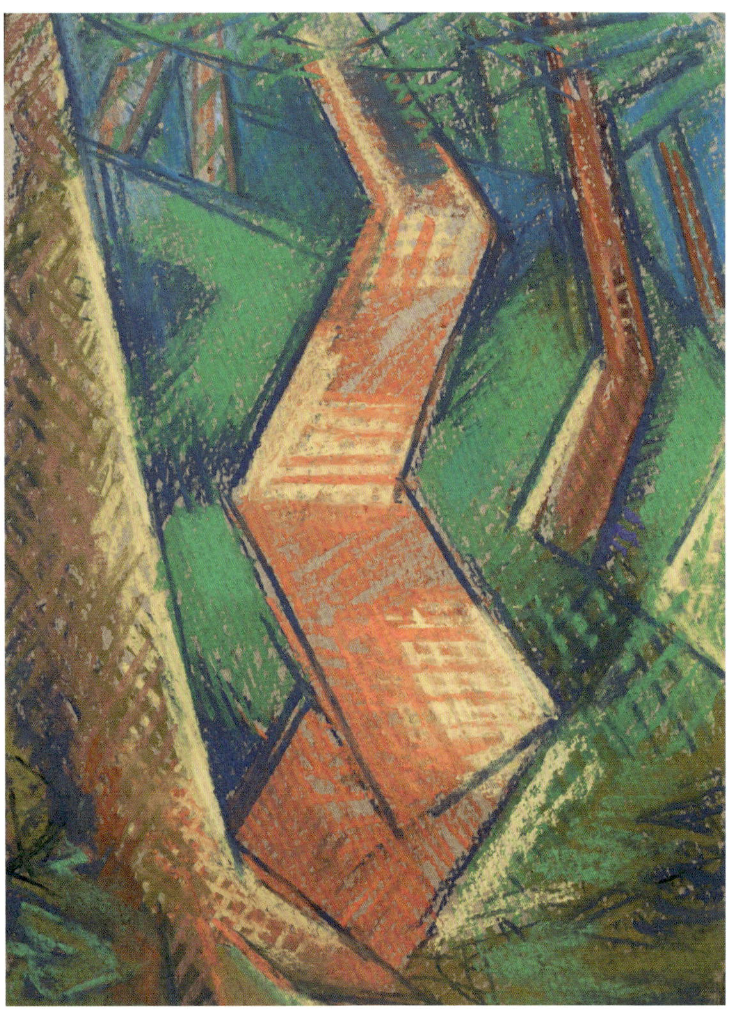

Andrew Lawson, *The
Path Through the Woods,*
2016. Pastel on Board

Right: Andrew Lawson,
The Red Path, Blue Stream,
2011. Oil on Canvas

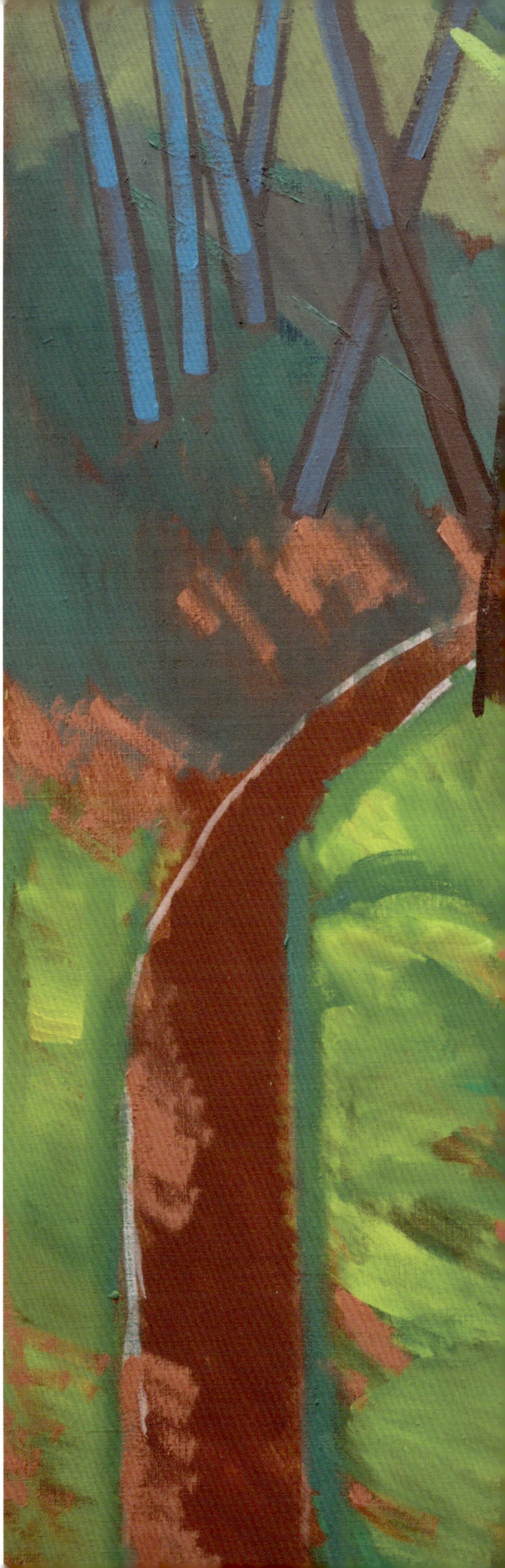

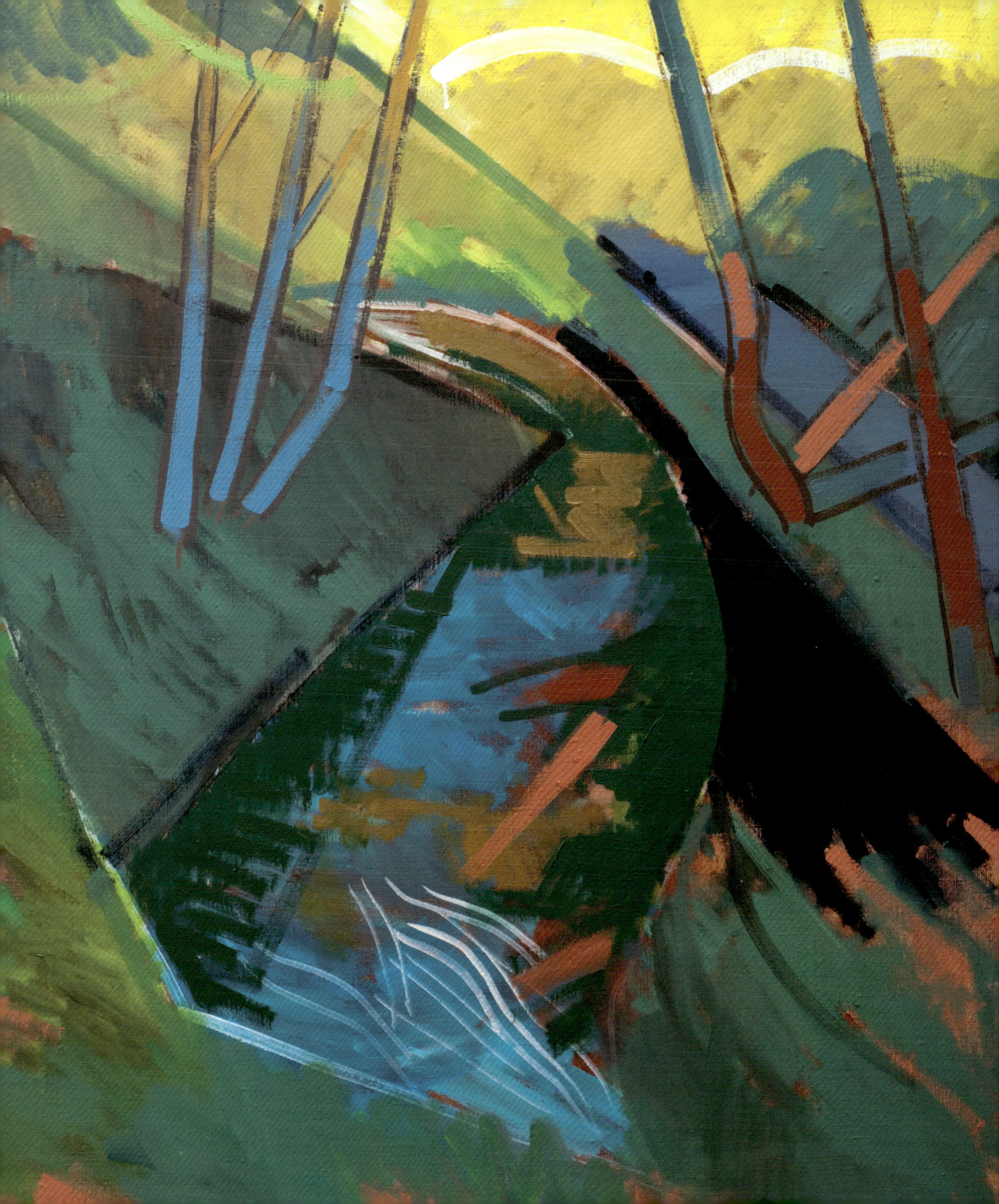

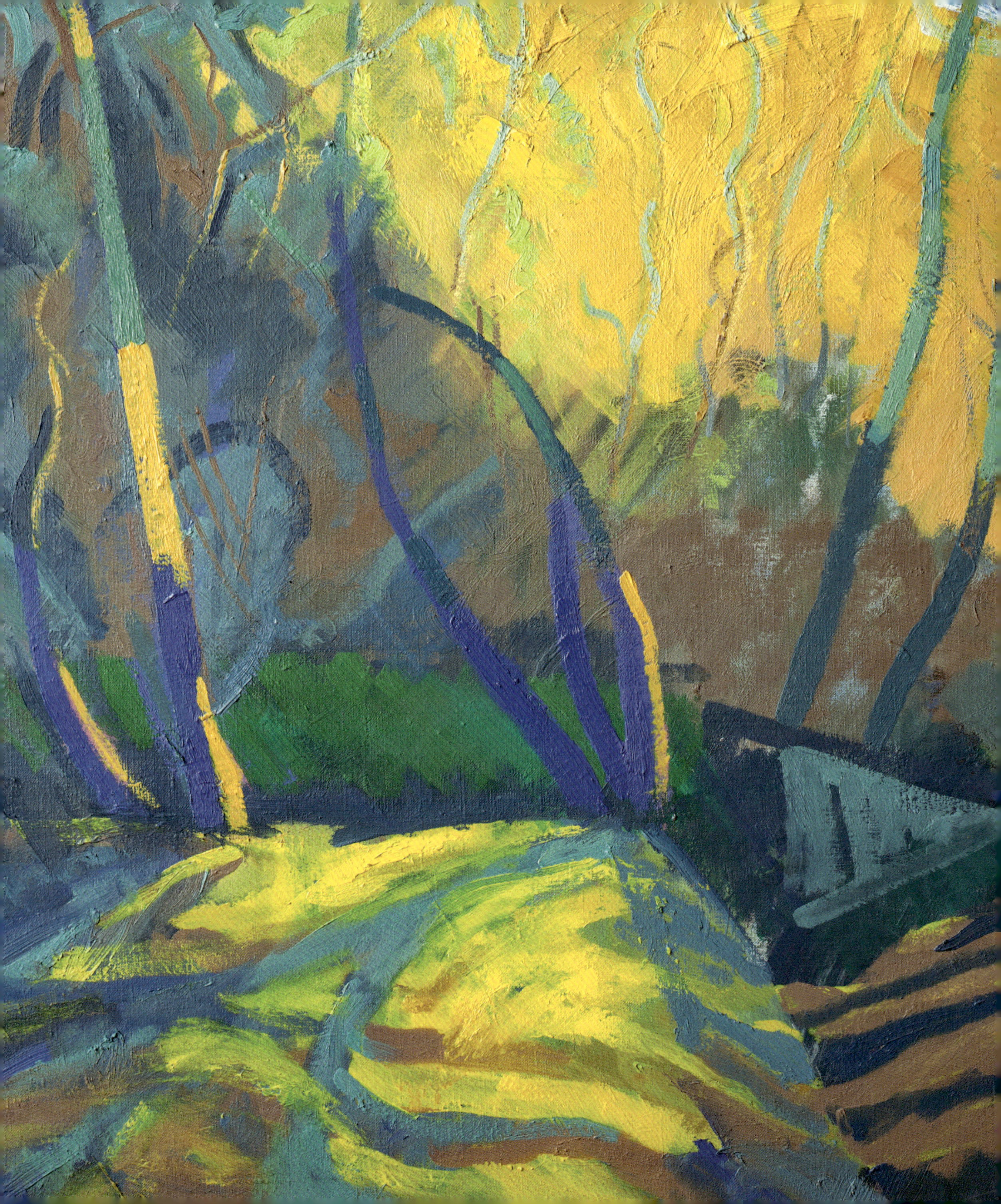

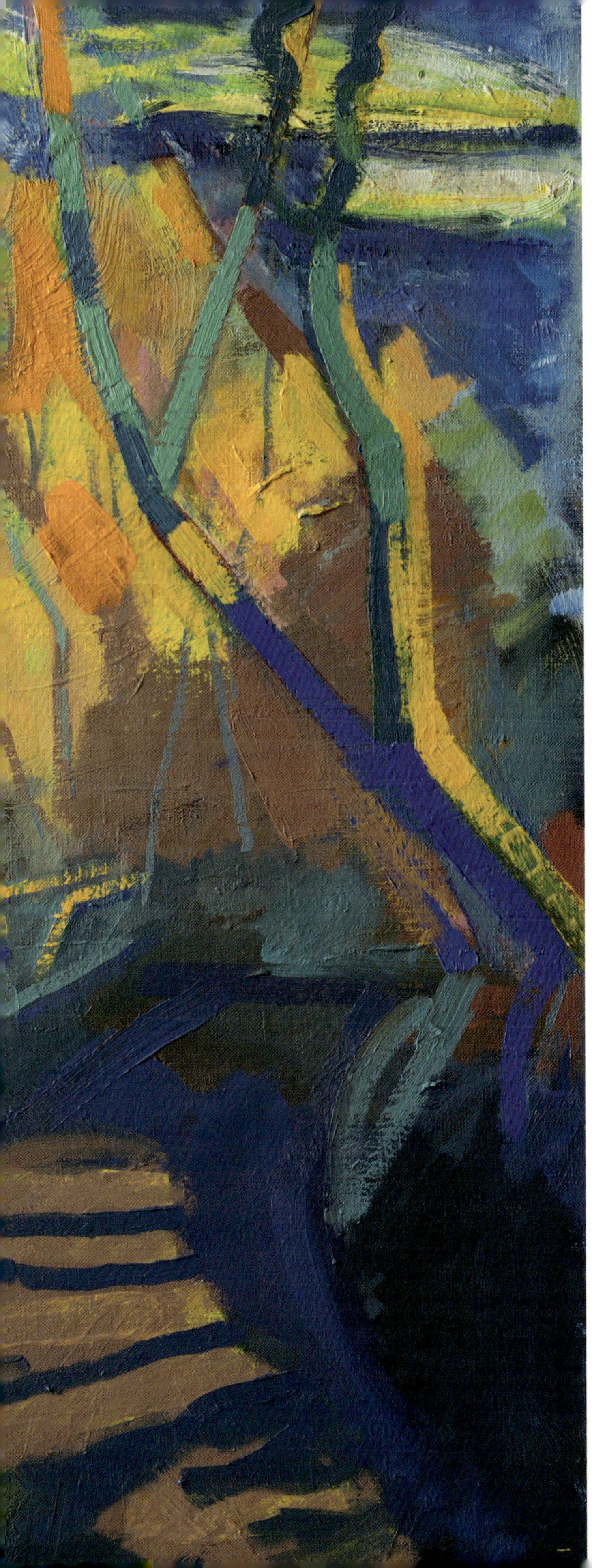

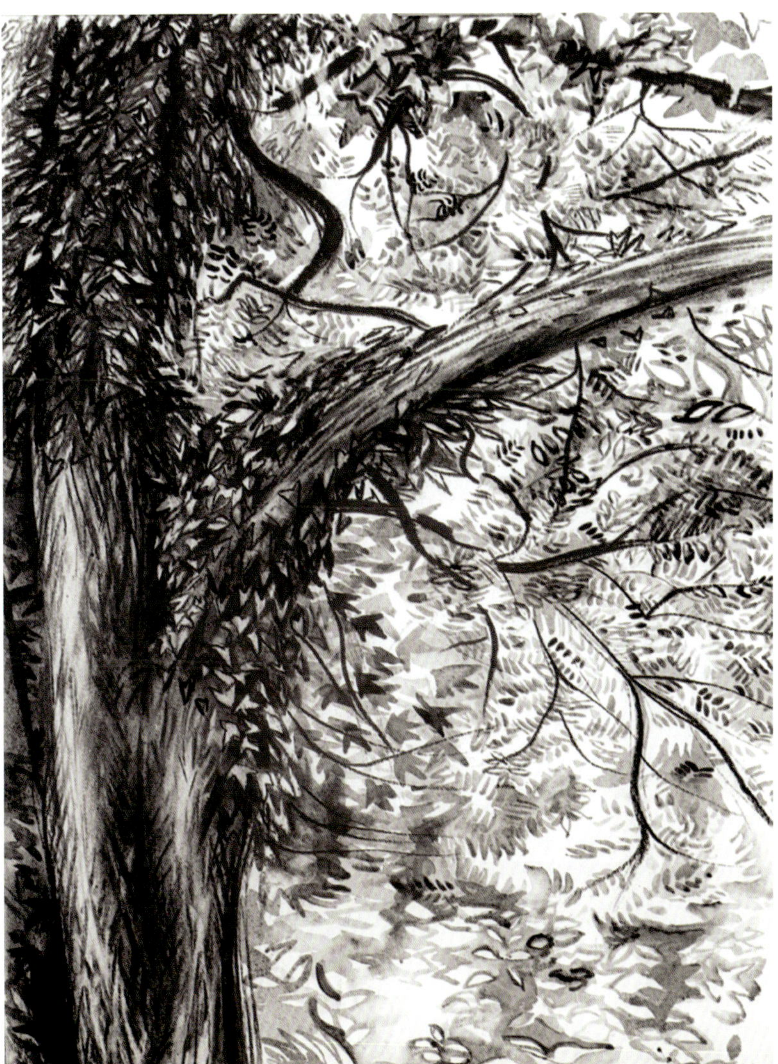

Above: Andrew
Lawson, *The Ash
Tree with Ivy*, 1976.
Charcoal

Left: Andrew Lawson,
Travelbridge, 2016, Oil
on Canvas

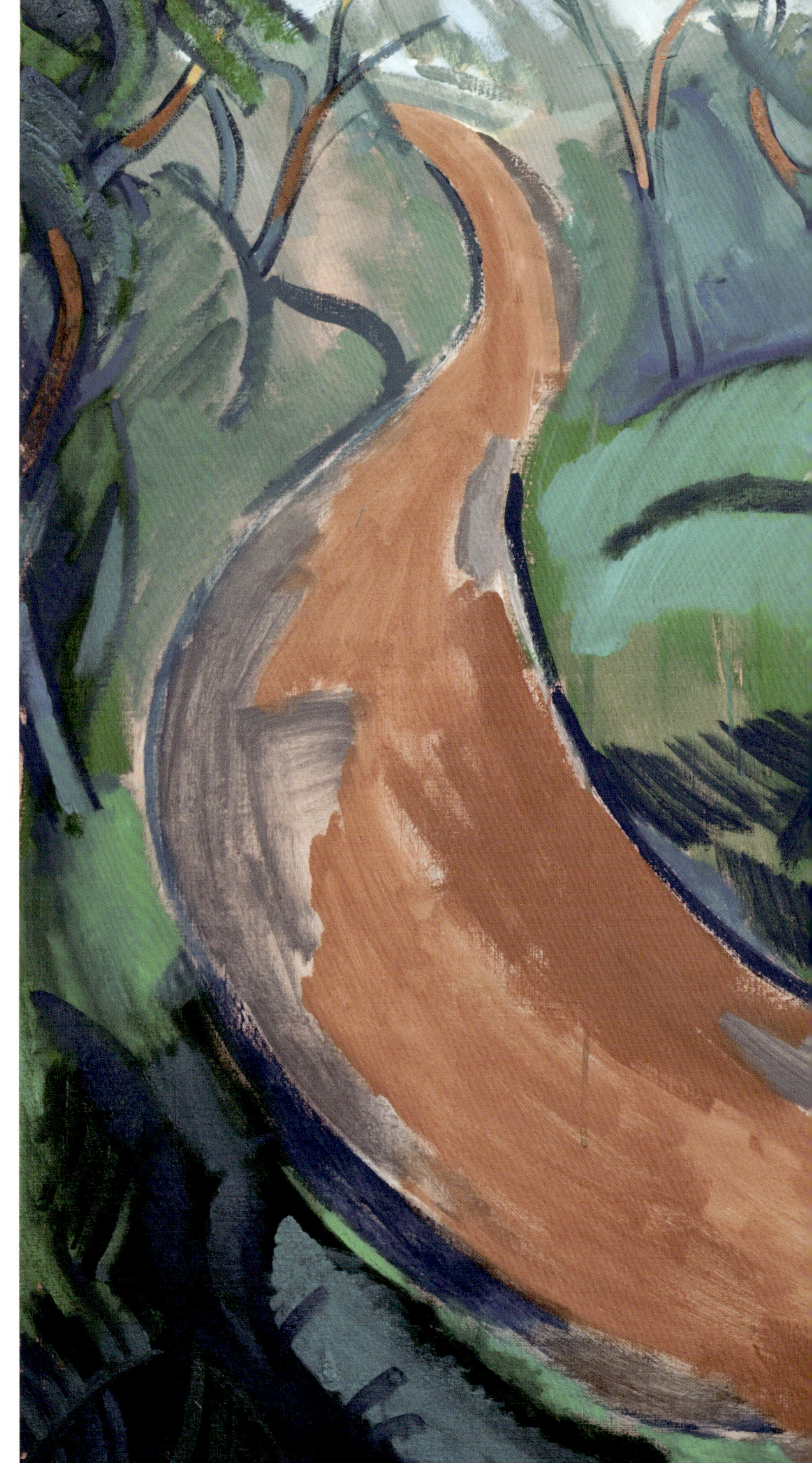

Andrew Lawson, *The Bend in the Track*, 2011. Oil on Canvas

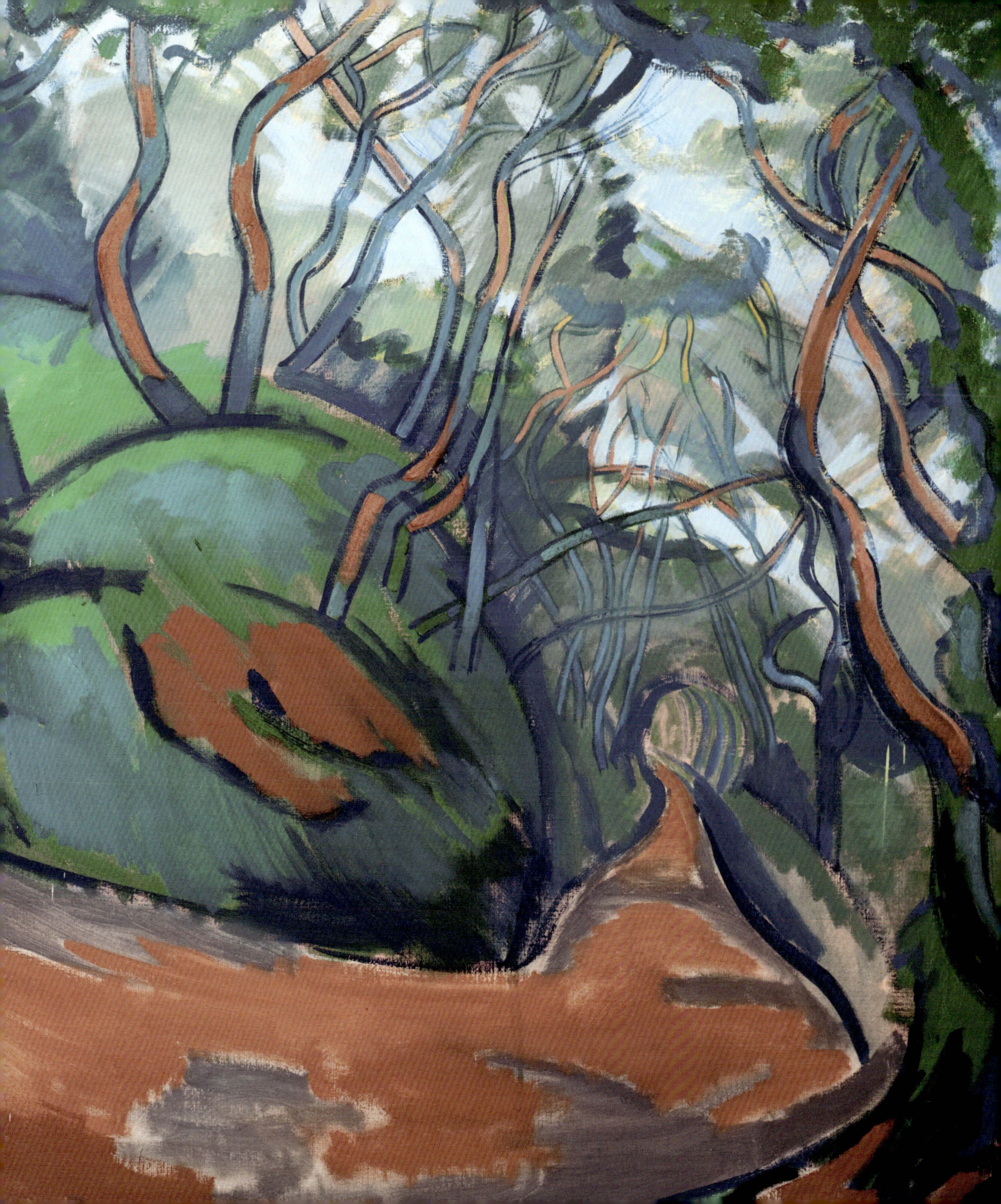

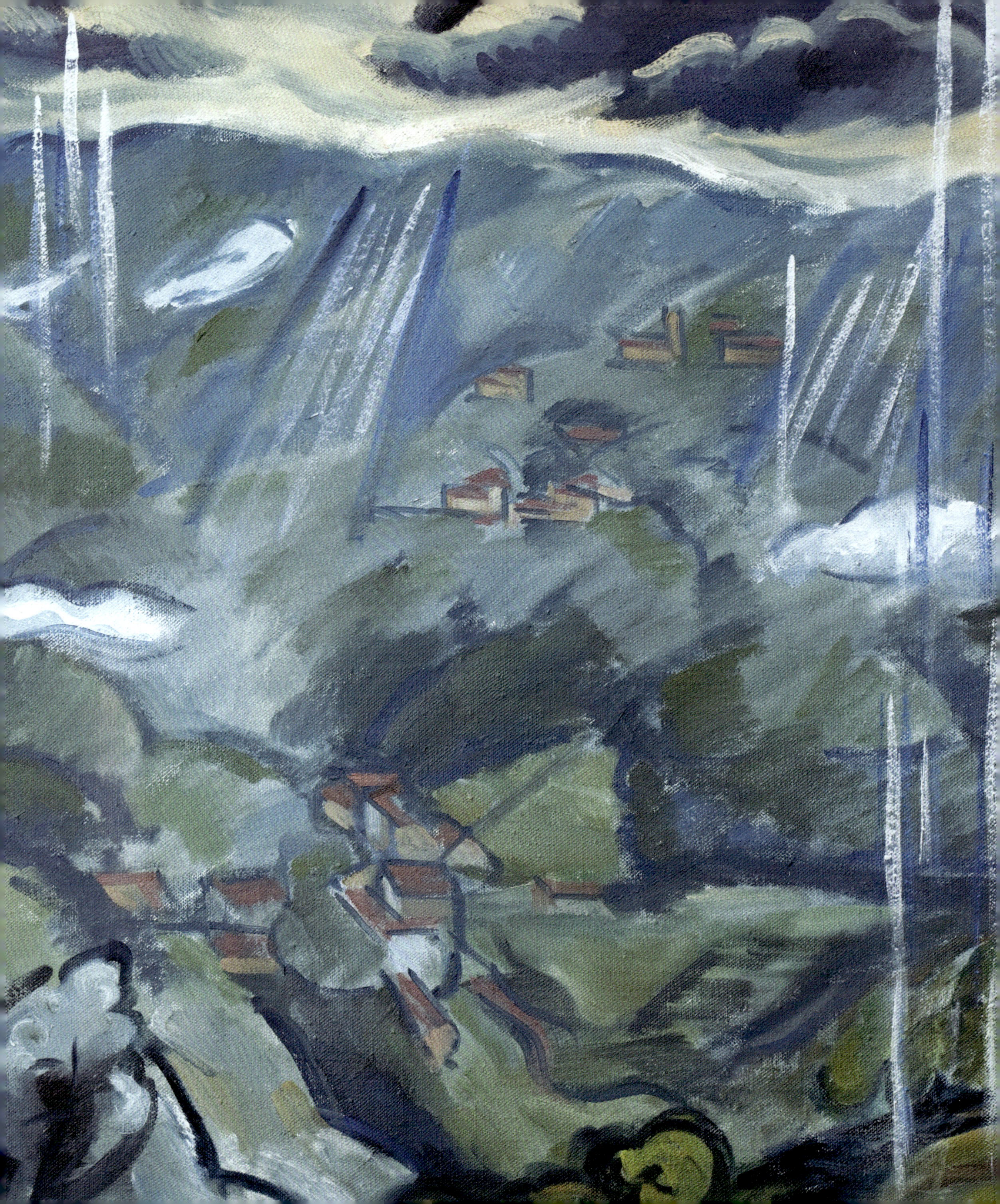

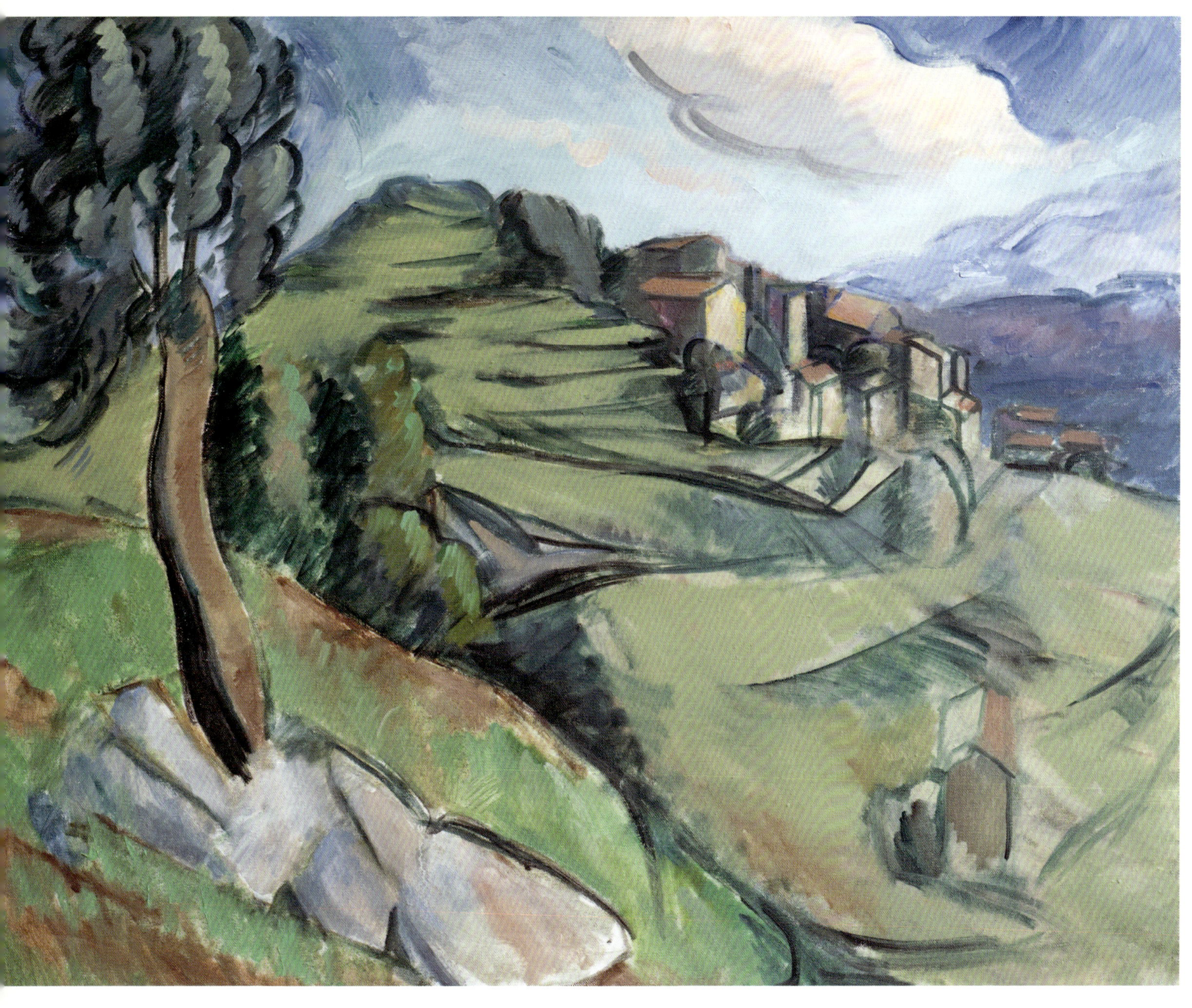

73

Andrew Lawson,
Castello, 2002. Oil on
Canvas

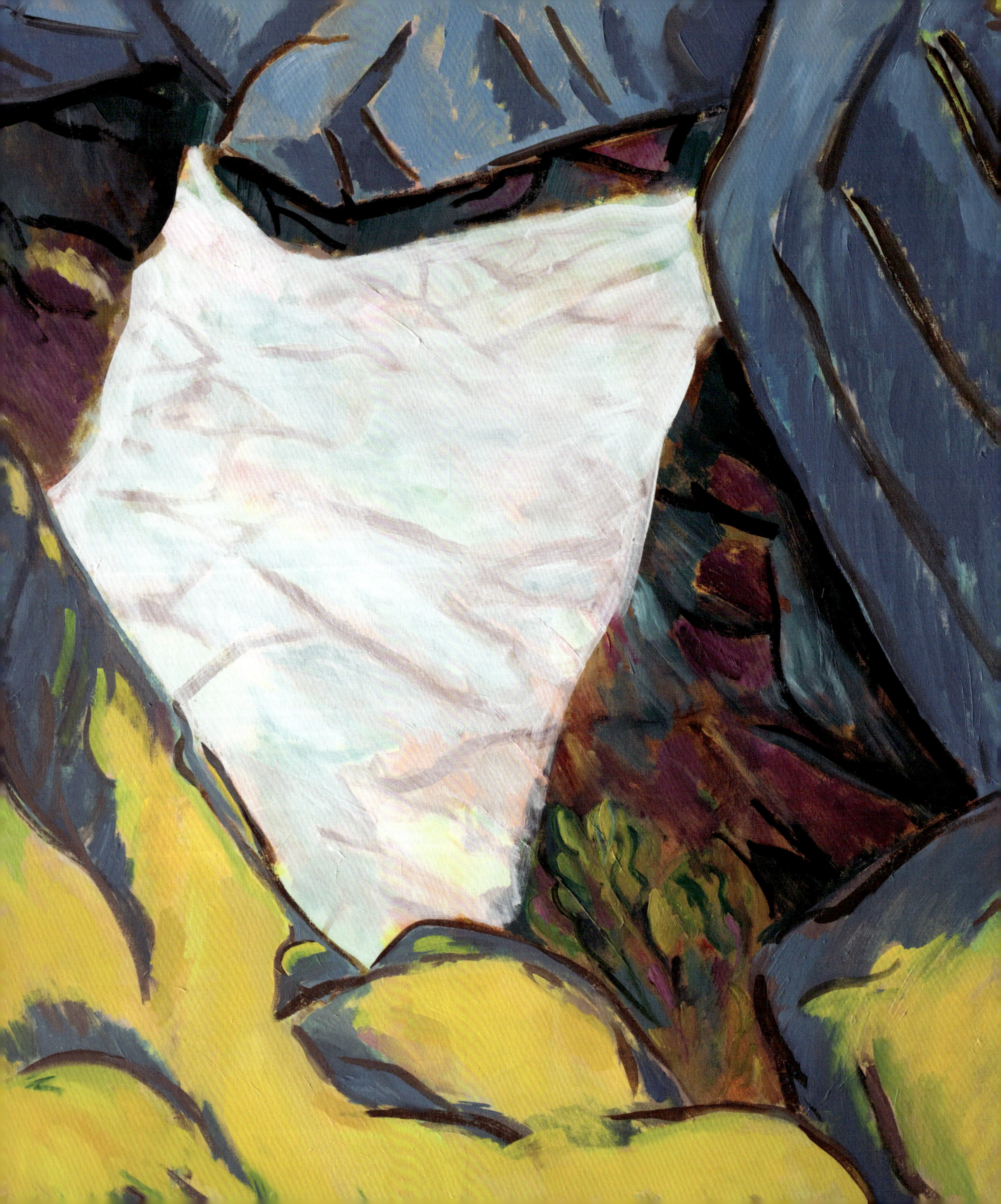

Left: Andrew Lawson,
Rockpool: Golden Rock,
2011. Oil on Canvas

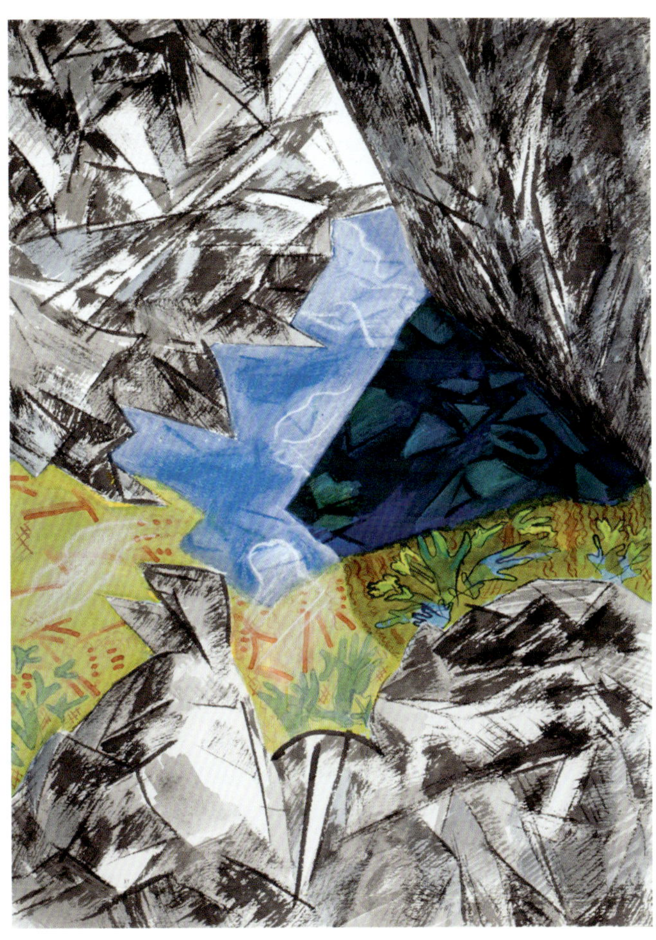

Andrew Lawson,
Rockpool: Jagged Rocks,
2011. Mixed Media
on Paper

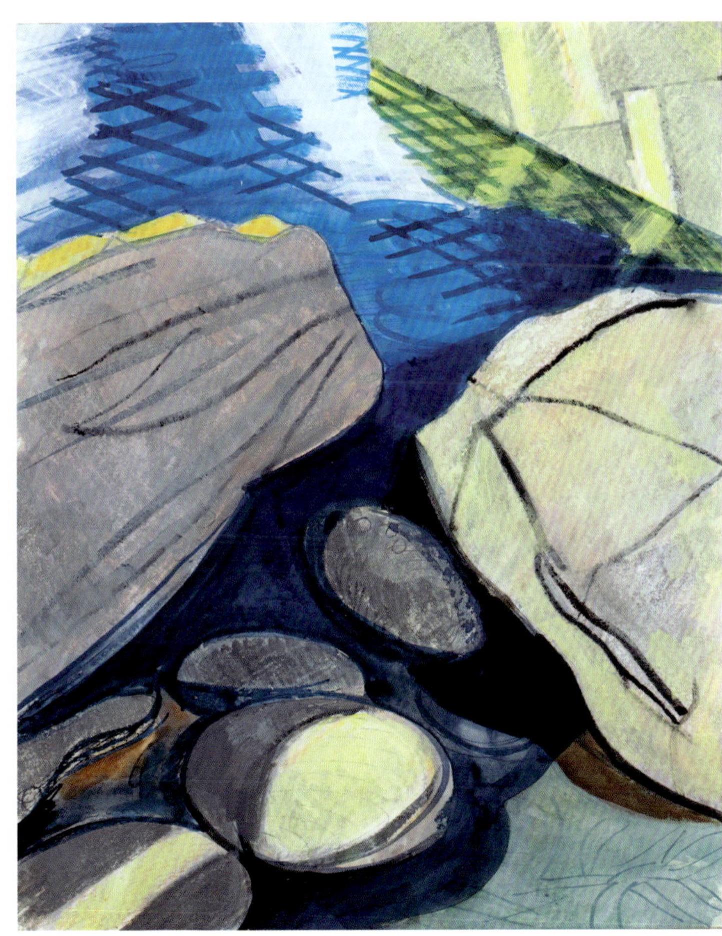

Andrew Lawson,
*Rockpool: Rounded
Rocks,* 2011. Mixed
Media on Paper

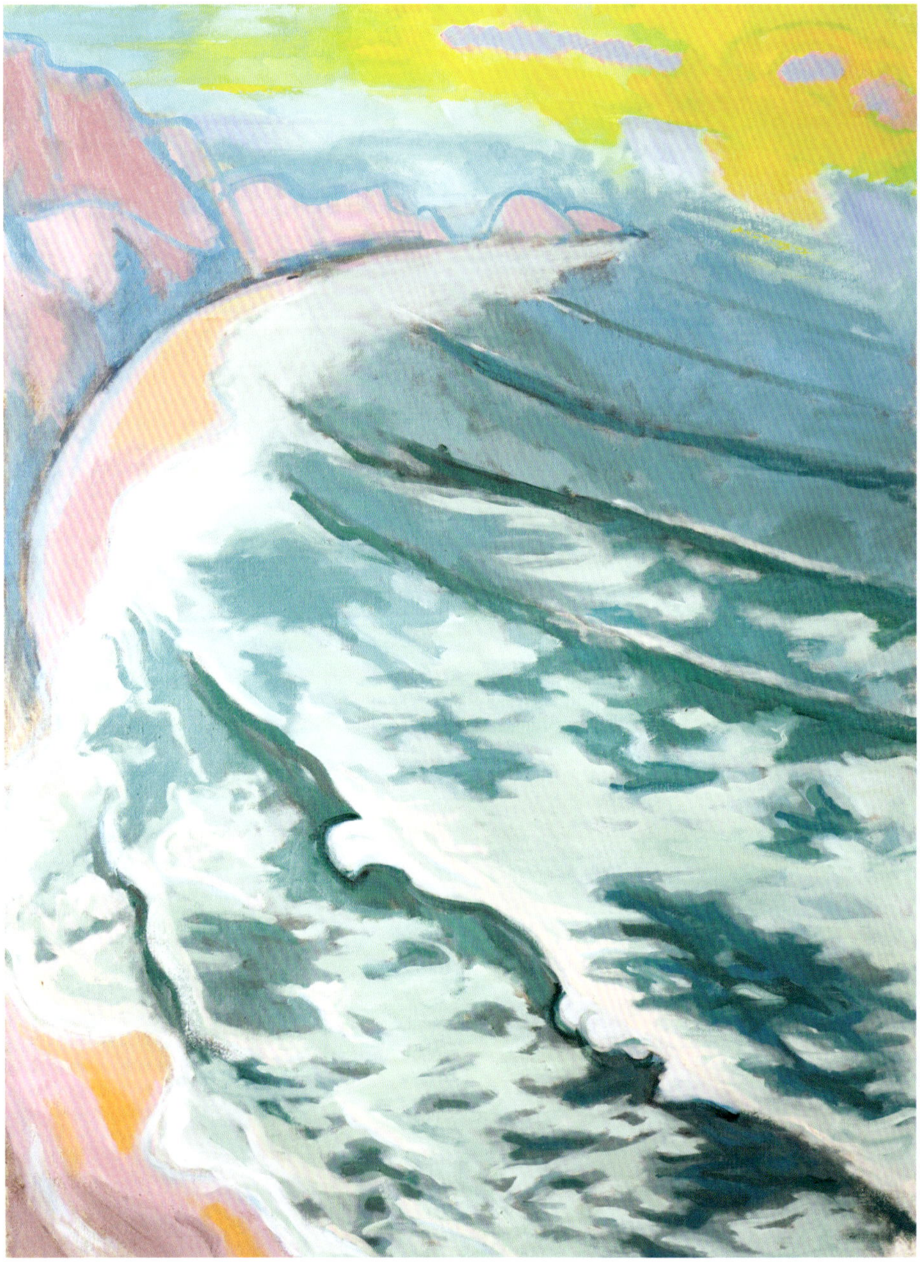

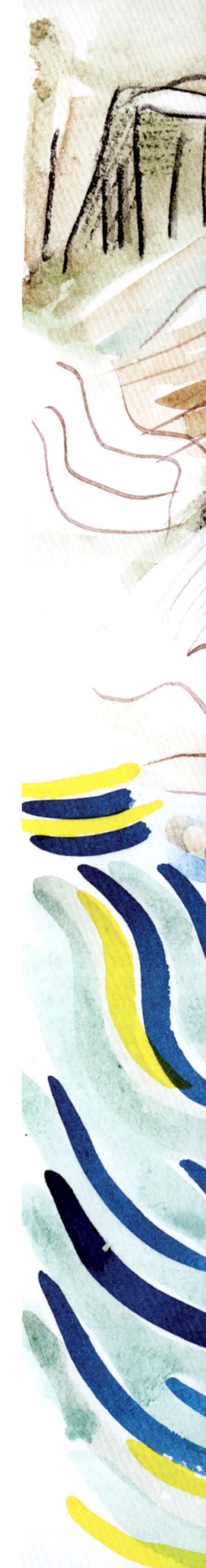

Andrew Lawson, *Sea
and Gull Rock*, 2011.
Oil on Canvas

Right : Andrew
Lawson, *The Marsland
Stream*, 2011. Mixed
Media on Paper

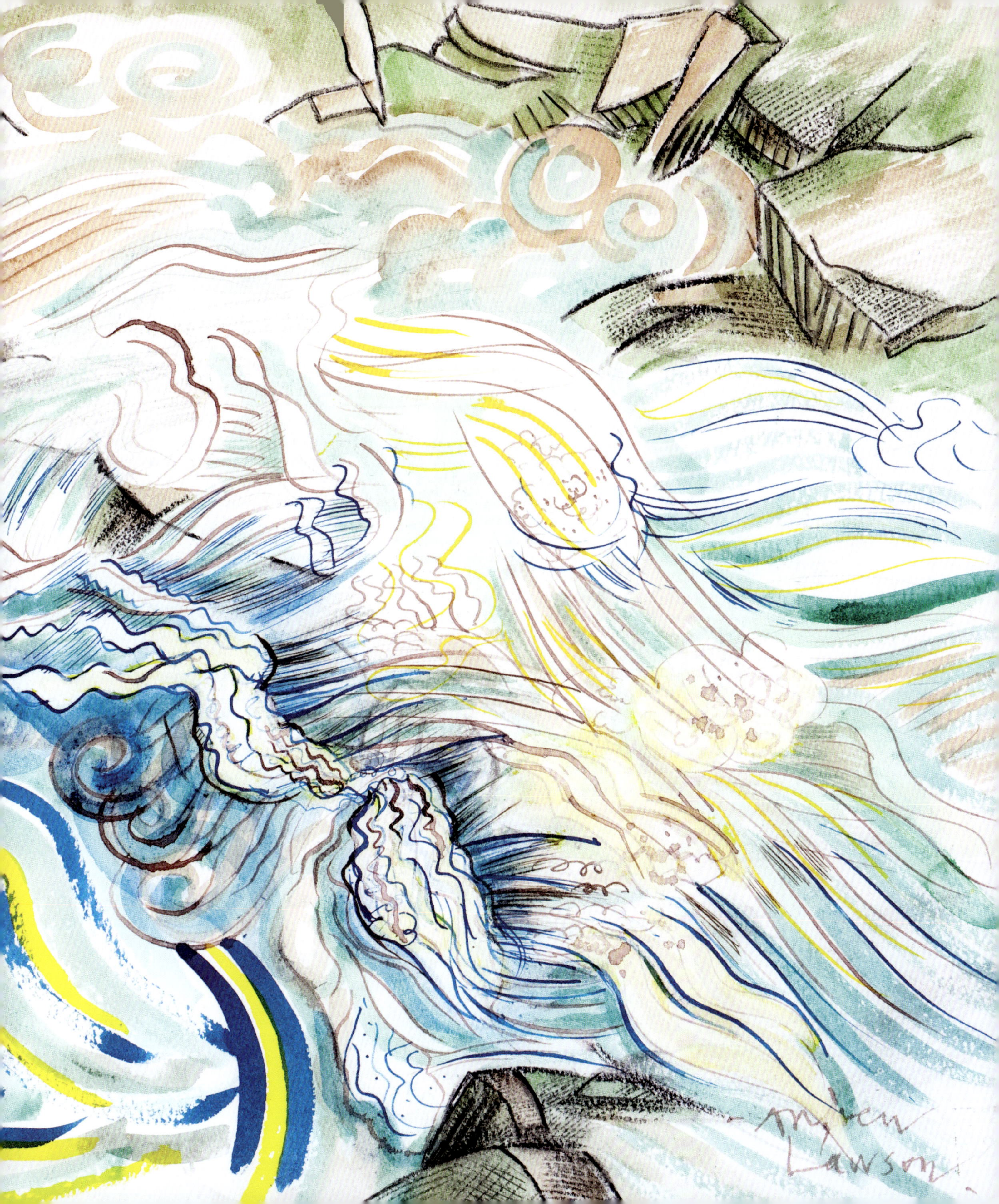

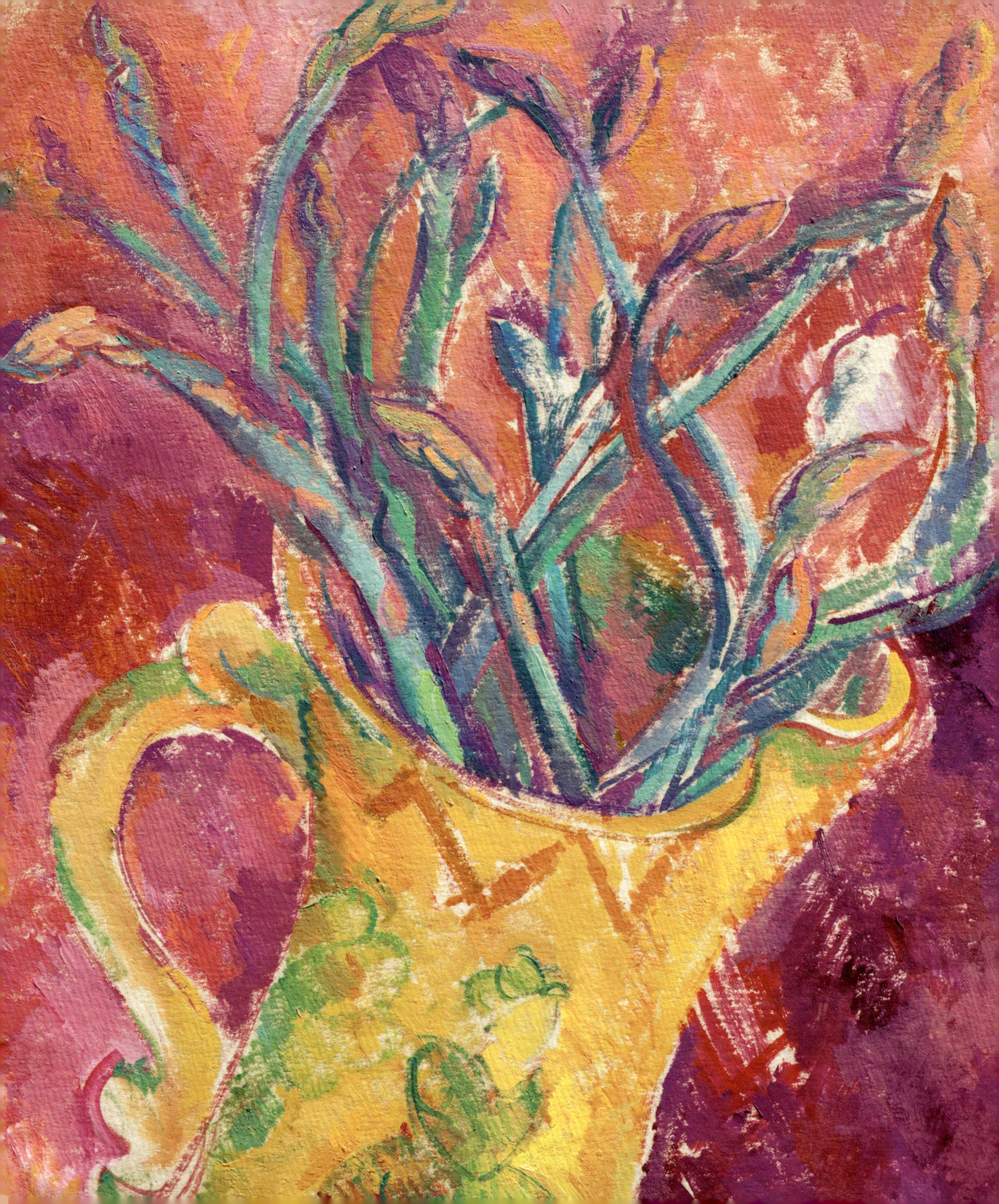

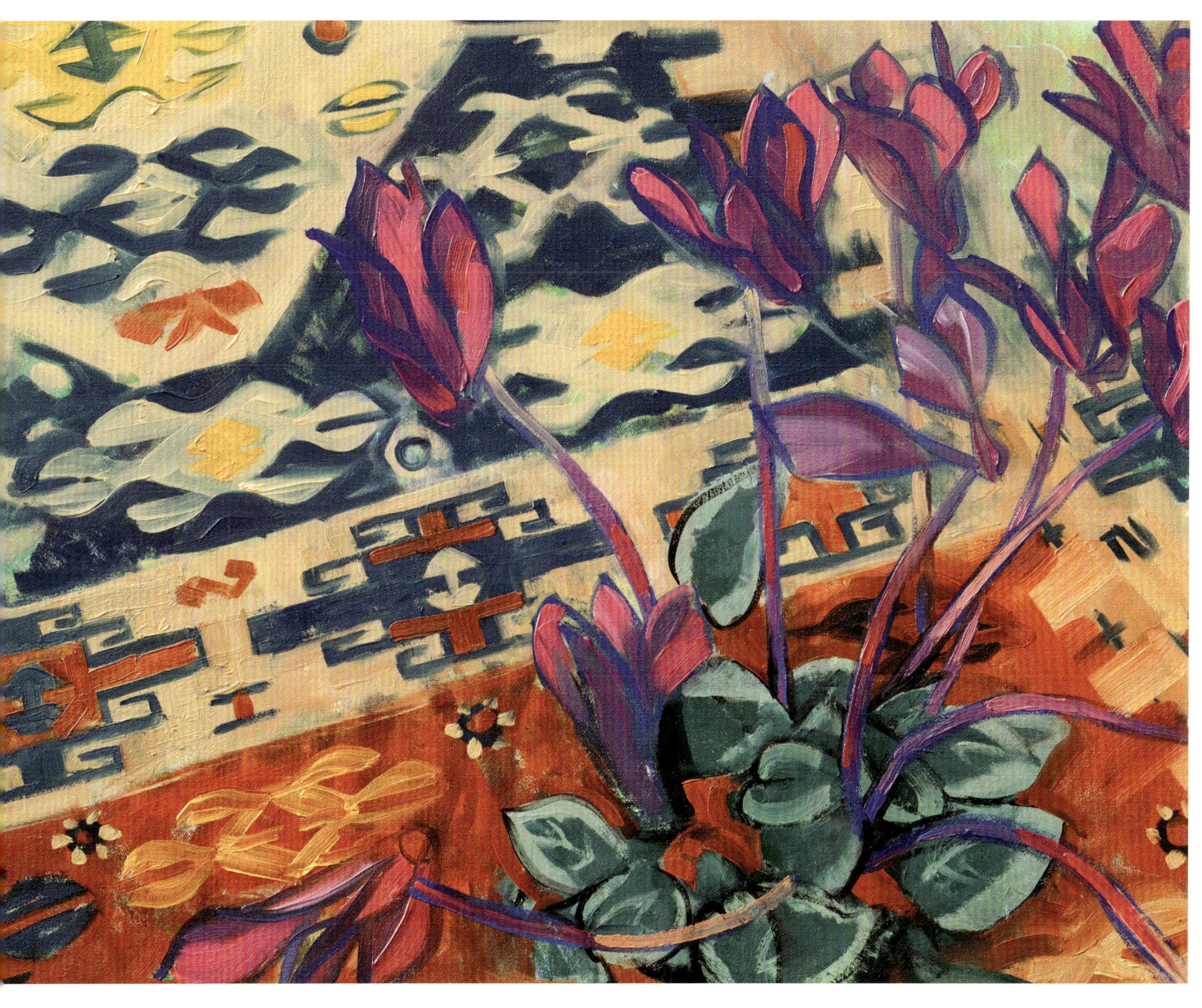

79

Andrew Lawson,
*Cyclamen and the
Soumak Rug*, 2011.
Oil on Canvas

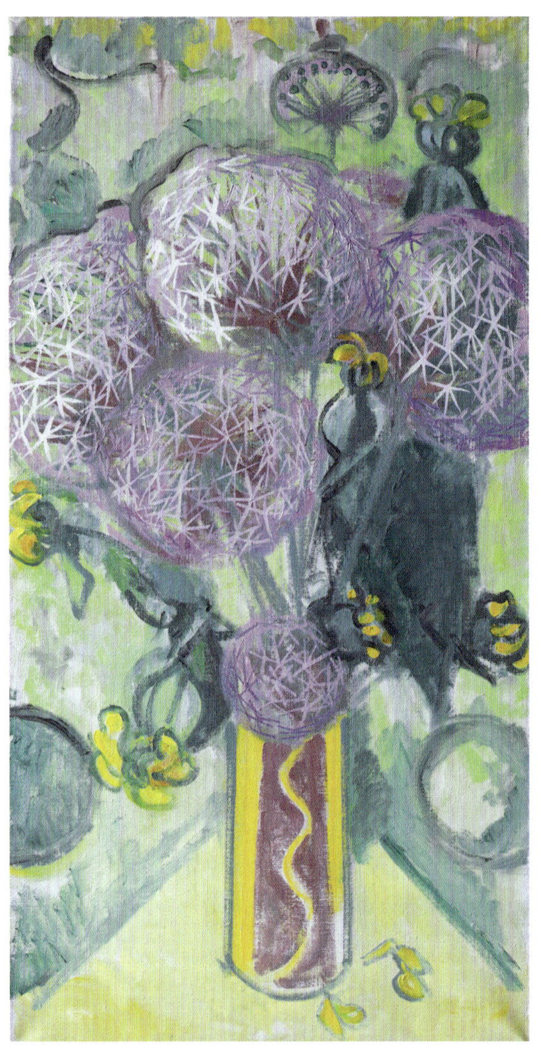

Andrew Lawson, *The Leach Pot with Alliums and Phlomis*, 2016. Oil on Canvas

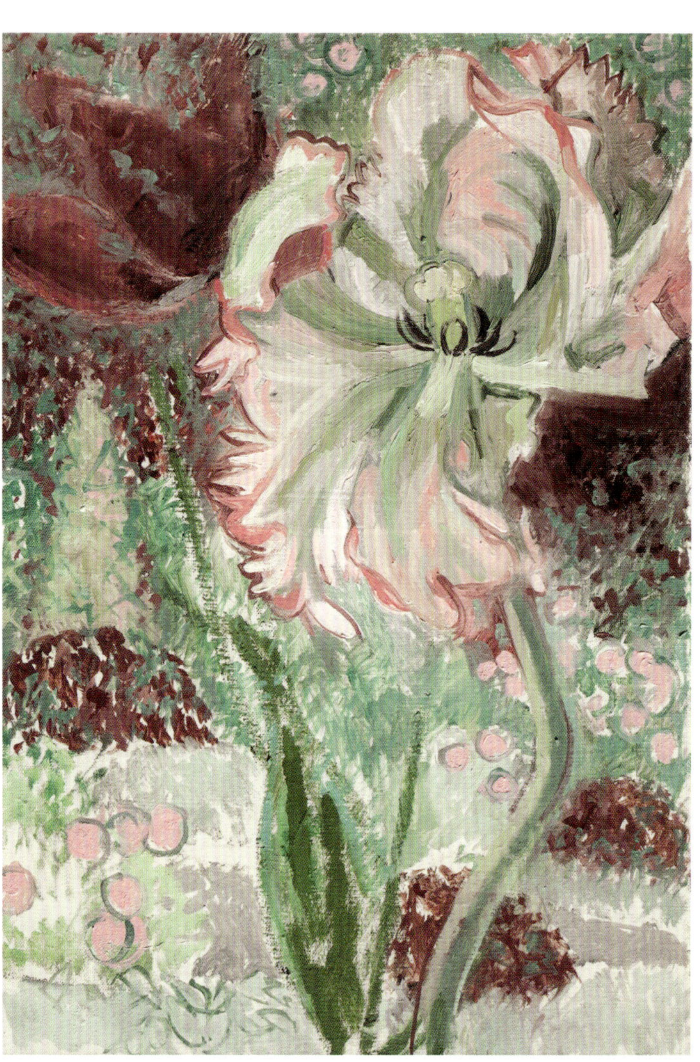

Andrew Lawson, *Parrot Tulip in the Garden*, 2016. Oil on Canvas

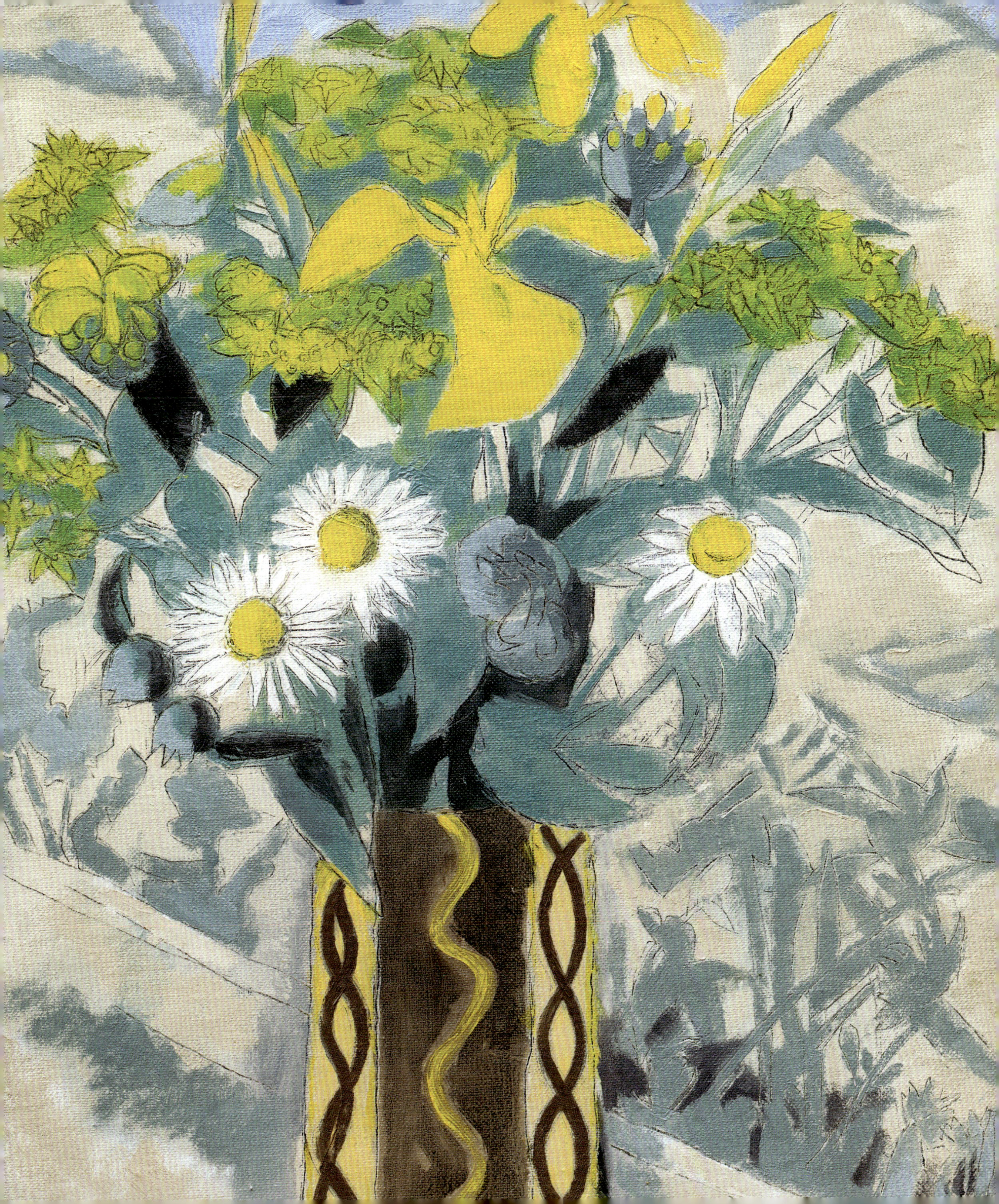

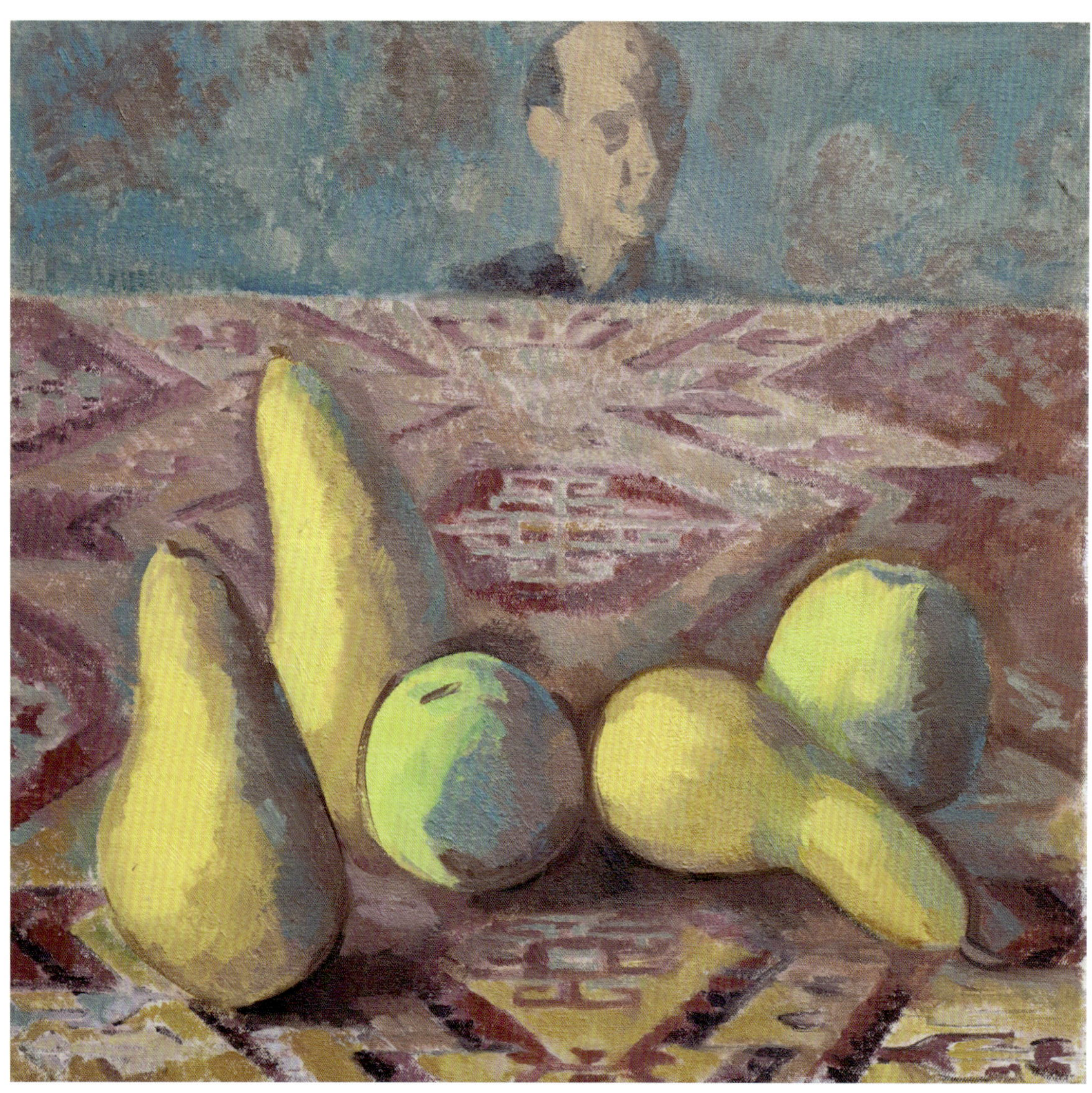

Andrew Lawson, *Pears
and Self*, 2007. Oil on
Canvas

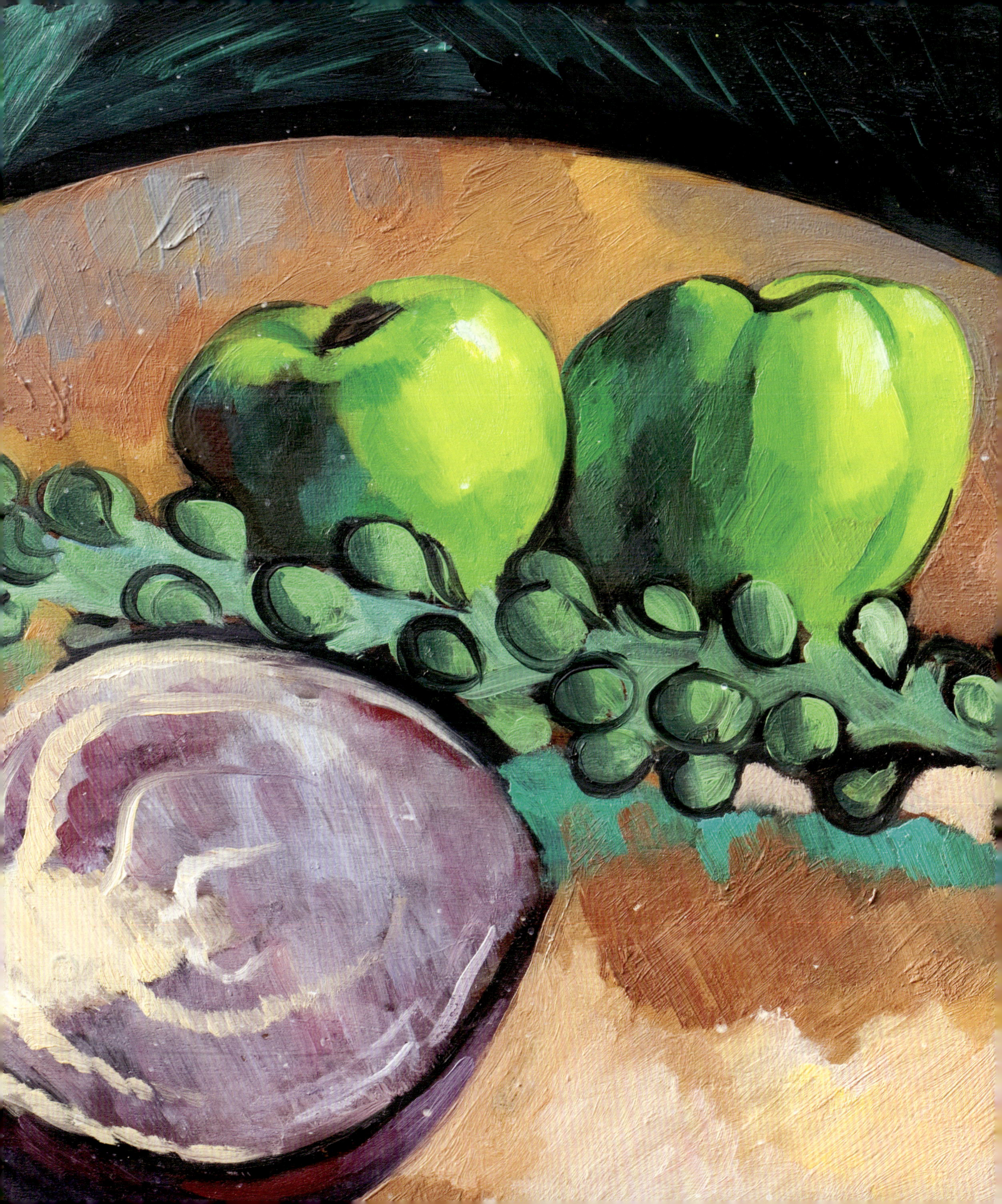

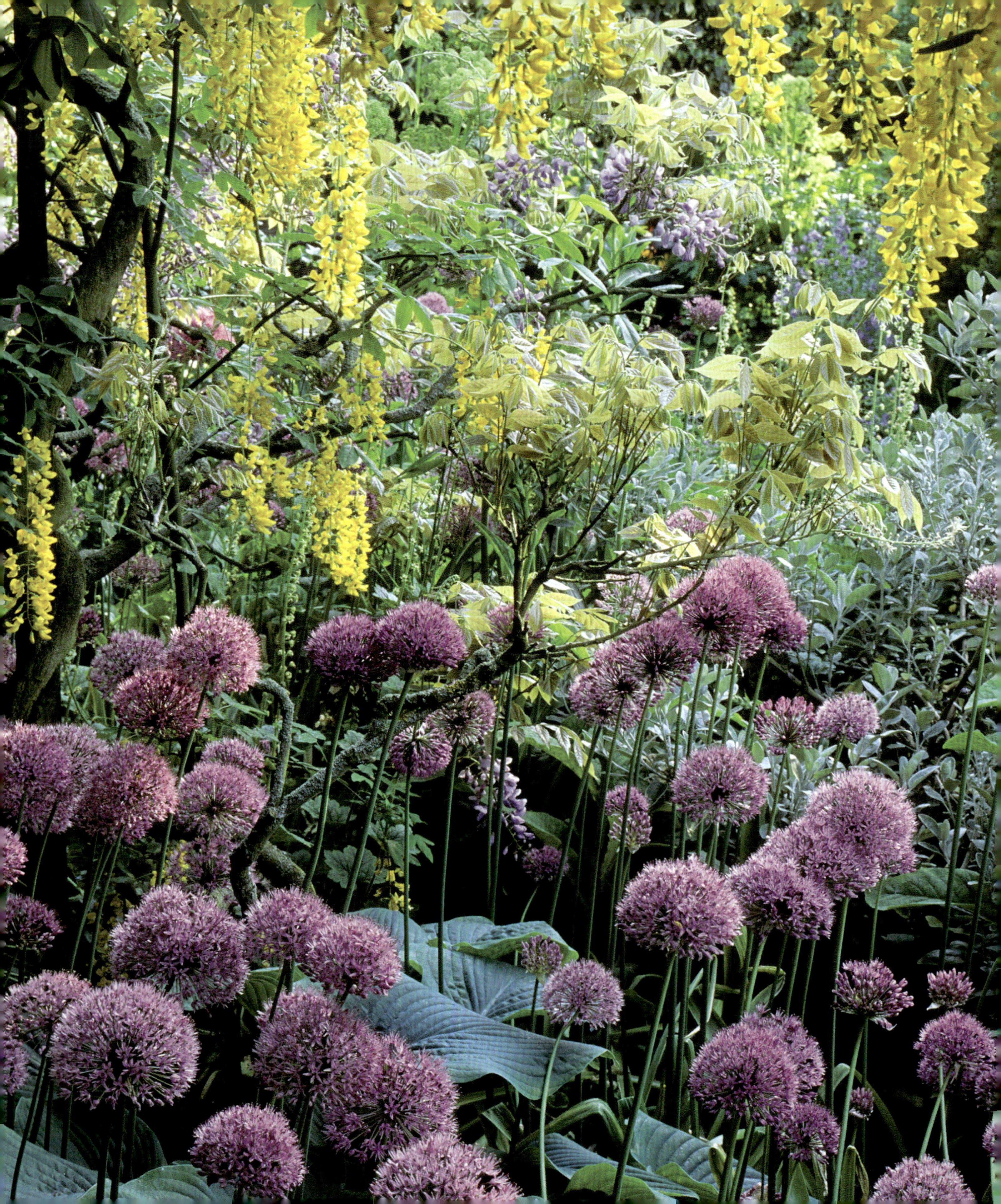

The Art of Gardens

by Andrew Lawson, 1990

I have been looking at paintings all my life, but I only started to look seriously at gardens quite recently when well into my middle-age. I find that familiarity with the language of painting is a useful background from which to view gardens. It does not seem to require a great quantum leap for the eye to adjust from a rectangle of pigments and forms arranged within a frame to coloured flowers and leaf shapes distributed upon the broader canvas of the garden.

I find that I now get the same thrill of pleasure from a good garden as I have always got from paintings that I admire. This pleasure is a cocktail of sensory delights, spiced with admiration for the skills of the artist. I confess that I have been moved to tears in admiration for gardens just as I have so many times in front of paintings.

I was struck by the close parallels between the arts of gardens and paintings by two casual remarks made to me and separated by twenty years. Freddie Gore, my painting tutor at St Martins, told me that 'Every artist has a limited range of colours to which he returns again and again'. Later, Rosemary Verey made more or less the same remark with reference to her planting: 'I know what colours work best for me' she said 'and I try to stick with them.'

Of all the gardeners I have known, Rosemary Verey was the closest to a painter in her attitude to colour. She used to pick a flower to hold against a prospective partner – like a draughtsman squinting to measure a model against the line of an outstretched pencil – and if she liked the association she would lift the plants and put them together without further ado. Once, when moving plants was impractical, she picked whole swathes of flowers from one patch of plants and threaded them among a complementary group, so that for a few hours one complete border was a glorified flower-arrangement, undetected by her visitors.

One colour association that worked especially well for Rosemary Verey was lilac-purple with pale yellow. She often chose to wear these colours herself, and so looked particularly harmonious in her own garden at Barnsley House. Her most triumphant celebration of purple and yellow is the famous laburnum walk there. Here the tall lilac-coloured globes of Allium hollandicum (aflatunense) rise to meet the hanging yellow racemes of Laburnum x vossii. It is a colour combination that finds further echoes in adjacent borders. These borders are a masterly statement of colour, of the kind that one might encounter in a Bonnard painting — but of course Bonnard never had to wrestle with the gardener's additional problem of orchestrating his colours to perform together at the same time.

As far as I can tell, Rosemary Verey's use of colour was intuitive, as it is with many artists, but her choice of colour combinations would have found favour with the Post-Impressionist painter George Seurat. Seurat was one of the great theorists of recent art, working as he did at a time when chemists and philosophers such as Chevreuil and Goethe had just revealed the physical basis for colour perception. They showed that certain colours could be regarded as diametrically opposite to other colours, which are called 'complementaries'. Red and green, for instance, are complementary, as are purple and yellow, blue and orange. Complementary colours provide the maximum available contrast. Nothing could be less purple than yellow. Green is the furthest one can go from red.

The effect of putting complementary colours side by side is the enhancement of each colour. A red looks all the redder for being put beside a green. Perception of purple is increased by an adjacent yellow. To see this effect, go from the laburnum walk at Barnsley House to the National Gallery in London and look at Seurat's painting 'Une Baignard' made in 1884 when the artist was 25. You will see that Seurat intensified a dominant colour by putting a touch of its complementary beside it. Wherever the blue of the water meets the flesh colour of the bathers, Seurat puts a few dots of orange pigment along the edge of the flesh. This intensifies the blue.

Just after the turn of the century a group of artists that included Matisse, Derain and Braque, were called 'Fauves' (wild beasts) by virtue of the intense colours that they used. Since then, the story of art has been a gradual unfolding of any remaining constraints on colour, form or materials. I would say that the reverse holds true in Garden Art, certainly in the field of colour. For sheer exuberance of pure colour in the garden we need to turn to the Victorian gardeners, or to their successors in our municipal parks and suburban gardens who maintain the Victorian tradition of annual bedding schemes. Their uninhibited use of pure colour for its own sake is sometimes derided by garden writers. Yet the brilliant bedding schemes of the best municipal parks are seen and enjoyed by more people than any other kind of garden, and without a doubt they lift the spirit of all who see them. Pleasure in pure colour can hardly be dismissed as unsophisticated. Rather, pure colour seems to satisfy a fundamental sensory urge.

In appreciation of art, the true art lover ignores fashion, for there is pleasure to be had from every smallest corner of the world of art. So it is with gardens. My advocacy of courageous colour partnerships does not prevent me from enjoying the more subdued colour schemes that we English seem to do so well. In painting, Gwen John and Ben Nicolson are, for me, quintessentially English artists – laid-back, quiet and refined, and Gertrude Jekyll is their gardening equivalent.

Monochrome plantings, like the hot borders at Hidcote, or the white gardens at Sissinghurst and Crathes, are the ultimate refinement of English 'good taste'. They correspond, if you like, to the drawings of the masters of art, limited in means, perhaps, but all the more revealing of the character and style of their creators. When you look at a border made up of plants of a single colour, your attention becomes all the more focussed upon the little distinctions of texture and shape.

Texture and shape take us into the realms of sculpture, and there are English gardens whose makers appear to have the sensibilities of sculptors of the land-scape. I am thinking of the late David Hicks, a brilliant architect and designer in other fields, whose garden in Oxfordshire had hardly a flower in sight. Instead he weighed one texture against another by interplantings of foliage plants, and one volume against another by carefully pruning his trees and hedges into solid-seeming structures. Rectangles of grass were allowed to grow long, framed by fillets of tightly mown grass for contrast. The trunks of a hornbeam hedge-on-stilts stand out against a background hedge of the same species.

Can there really be such a thing as a cubist garden? Cubism, you remember, was one of the most revolutionary movements in 20th century painting, initiated by Picasso and Braque around 1907, and subsequently insinuating an influence on much painting up to the present day. Expressed simply, cubism represented a new way of seeing the world – fragmented and viewed from several angles at the same time; a world split up into compartments of space and time. And what does that remind you of? Why, Hidcote, of course, the most revolutionary and influential English garden of the 20th century. It seems to me more than a coincidence

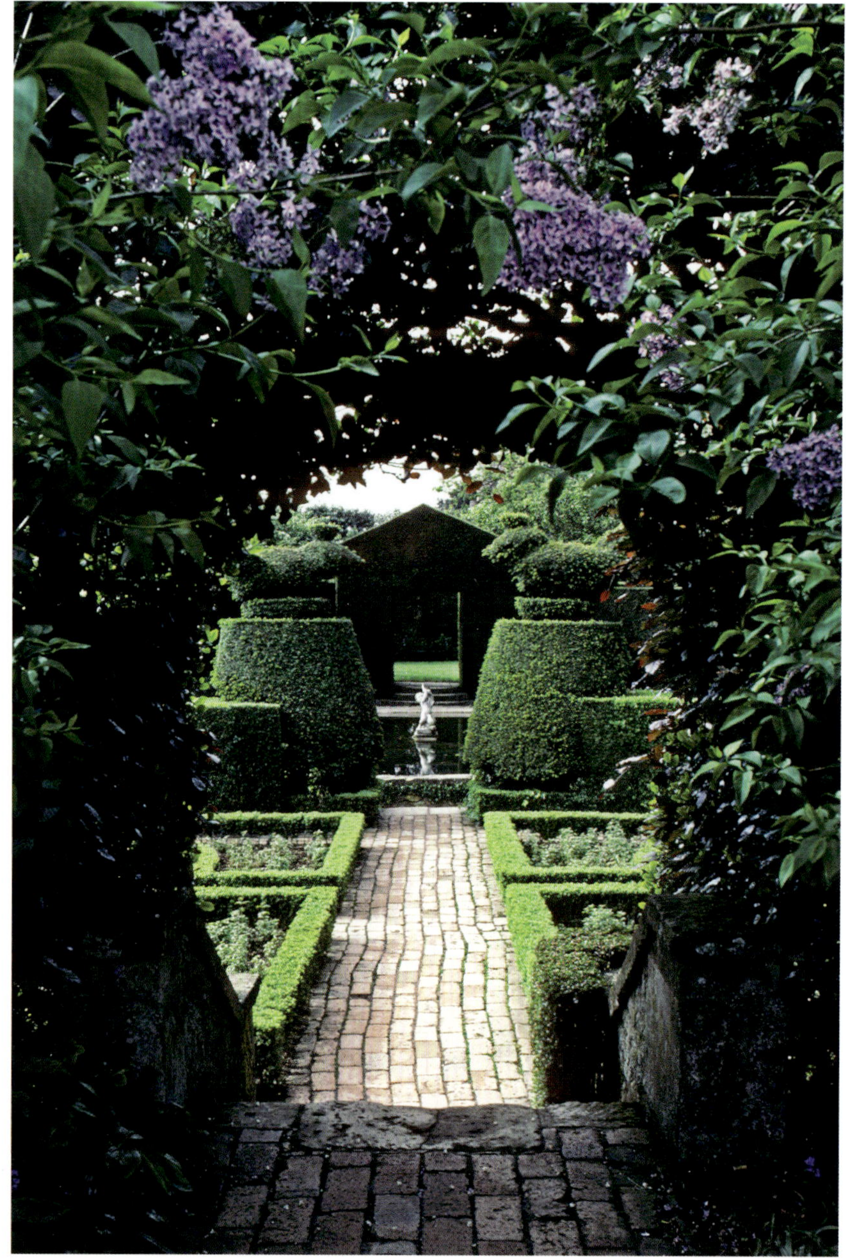

Hidcote : through
lilacs to the Fuchsia
Garden and the
Bathing Pool

that Hidcote was also created from 1907, the year that Lawrence Johnston first moved into the Manor and began to make his garden. I am not suggesting that Johnston knowingly created a cubist garden, or even that he was aware of what Picasso and Braque were up to in Paris. It may just be an instance of a new idea, when its time is ripe, appearing in several places at the same time, as so often happens with discoveries in science.

Having given you a cubist garden, my next trick is simple – a surrealist one. The surrealist, like Dali and Magritte, enjoyed delivering a shock to the spectator by putting together familiar things in an unfamiliar way. My favourite surrealist garden was knowingly surreal. It was created by Lord Berners at Faringdon House. In a pool in front of the Orangery reposes a solemn bust of the Victorian dignitary Sir Henry Havelock. The water laps around his shoulders. He looks like a seal coming up for air. In the dovecote nearby the living birds have been dyed magenta, lemon and blue like so many boiled eggs on Easter morning. And a blue dog lurches around the garden. It is all a great joke. And why should a garden not be funny?

The English are inveterate collectors of things, and many a garden is a depository of some arcane collection or other. When you visit Stowe you get the impression that the Temple family collected temples like you or I might collect paperweights or First Editions. I know a garden in Cornwall which contains a collection of cast iron Victorian kitchen ranges, all proudly polished and burnished. Garden gnomes are another example of this collecting phenomenon – the Gnome Reserve in Devon occupies over an acre of woodland in which hundreds of gnomes frolic in every imaginable activity.

The French painter Claude Lorraine remarked that there are only two branches of the Fine Arts – painting and pastry-cooking. That may be the case for the French. For the English, I like to think that there are two Fine Arts too – painting and the creation of gardens. Of the two, I would say that we are lucky enough, through climate and inclination, to excel at the latter. Such is the abundance and diversity of our gardens that one could spend a lifetime absorbing the artistry that they have to offer.

Reprinted from Hortus

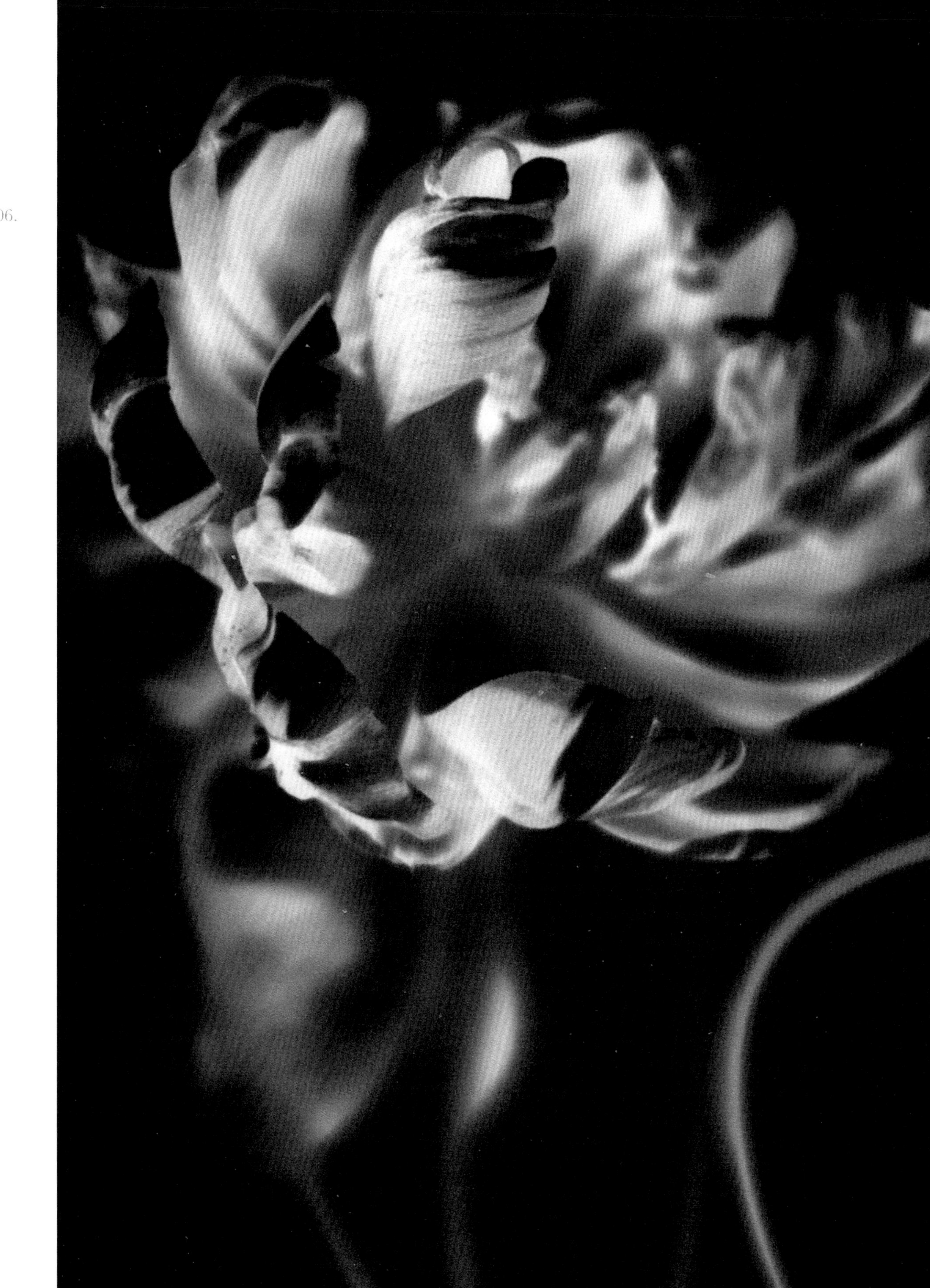

Left : Andrew Lawson, *Tulip*, 2006. Photograph

Monochrome photography

Andrew Lawson

I suppose that I must belong to one of the last generations that saw the world in black and white. Black and white movies and television. Black and white newspapers. And a whole history of earlier photography that had been almost exclusively monochrome.

Black and white photographs were all we knew. But in our imaginations we learnt to add the missing ingredients of space, of three dimensions and yes, of colour. We learnt to look and to interpret. A black and white image became a template on which our imaginations became engaged.

Over the last 30 years I have made approximately 300,000 colour images of subjects related to gardens. A number of these have been used to illustrate books and magazines. 'Illustrate' is the operative word here. In an illustration of a garden, the element of colour is essential. Unless you are shown the colours of a particular garden it would be impossible to imagine them.

A colour photograph is generally made for the purpose of showing the subject in reality, or as close to reality as possible. In making a colour photograph of a garden I have felt that I am making a record of the artistry of the garden-maker, as well as an ephemeral moment. Any 'art' in the garden photograph is contained in the subject. The photographer's contribution is to catch the subject at the right time, and to choose the optimum viewpoint. These are considerable skills, of course, but they give very little scope for interpretation. And for the viewer of the picture, everything is offered on a plate and the imagination is hardly engaged.

With monochrome photography, there is much more scope for interpretation and imagination, both on the part of the photographer and of the viewer. There is less demand on the photography to be realistic. The photographer has liberty to adjust reality, and the viewers to engage their imaginations.

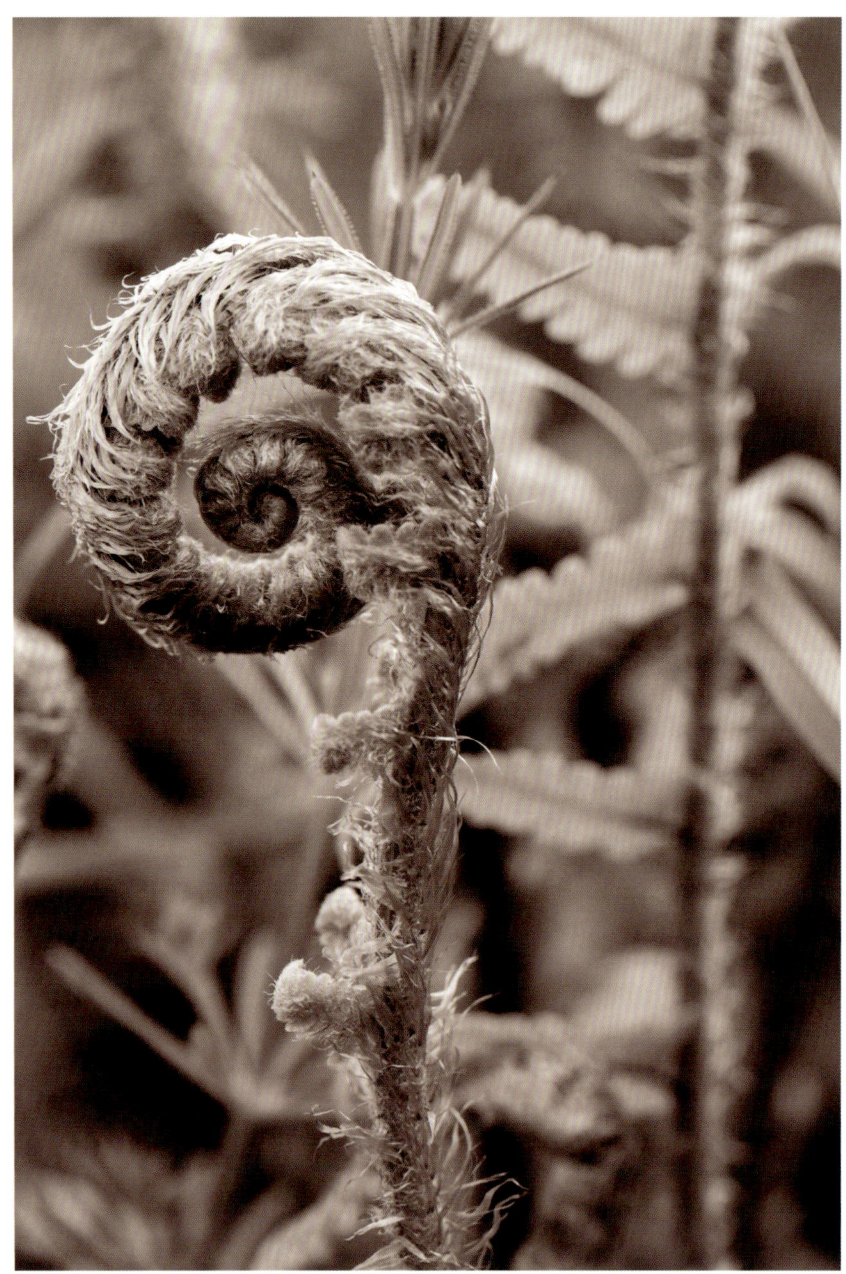

Andrew Lawson,
Crozier, 2001.
Photograph

92

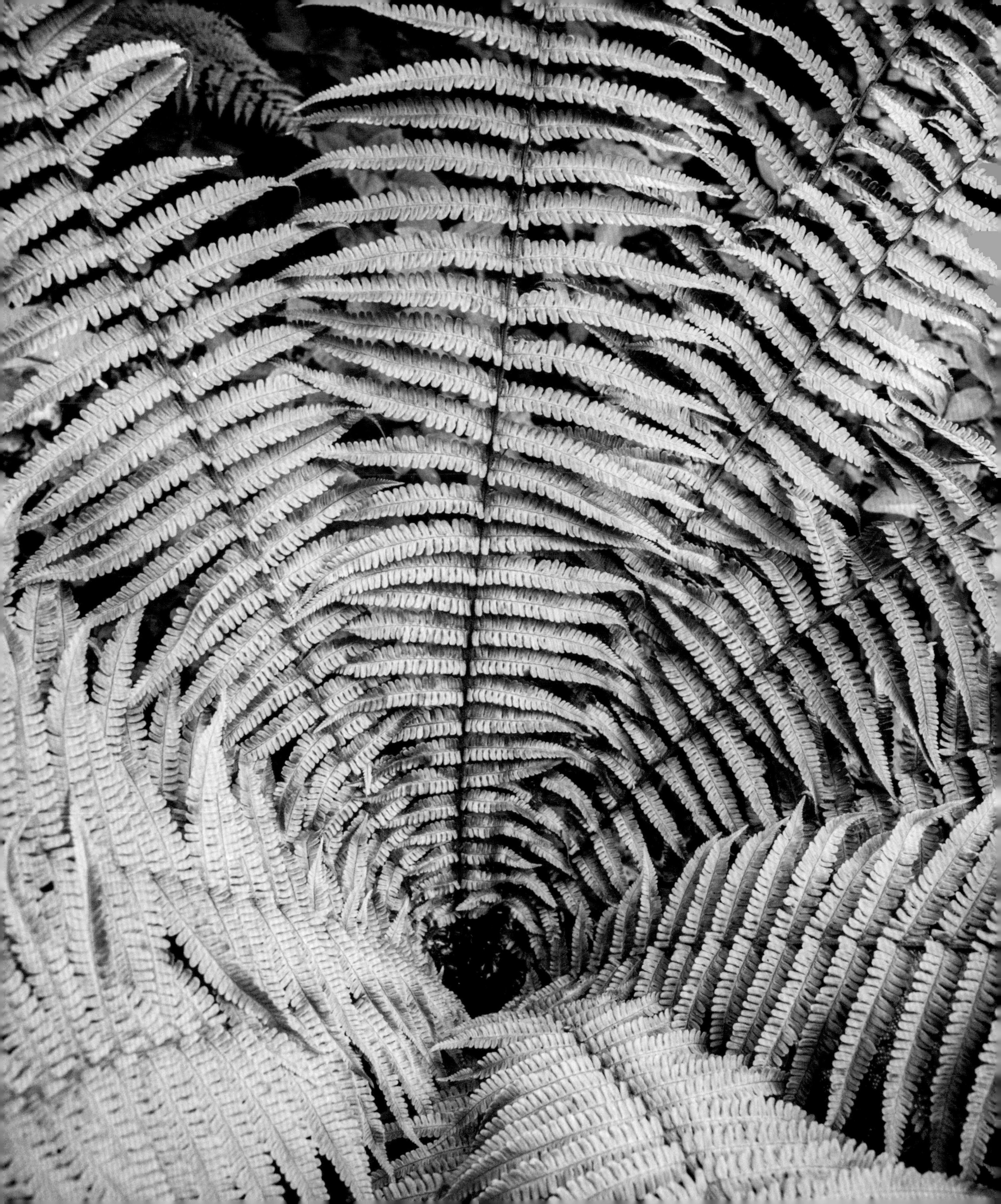

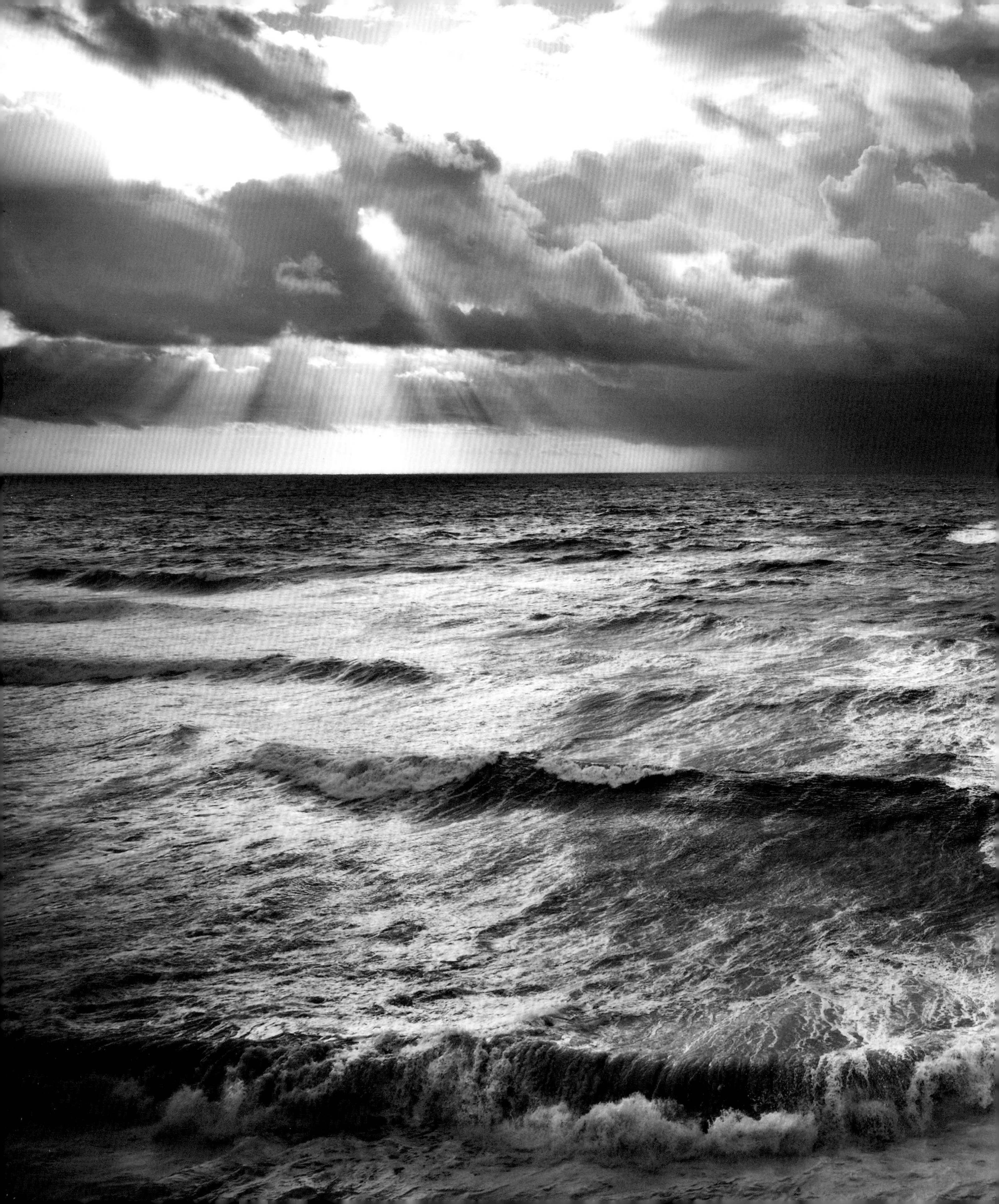

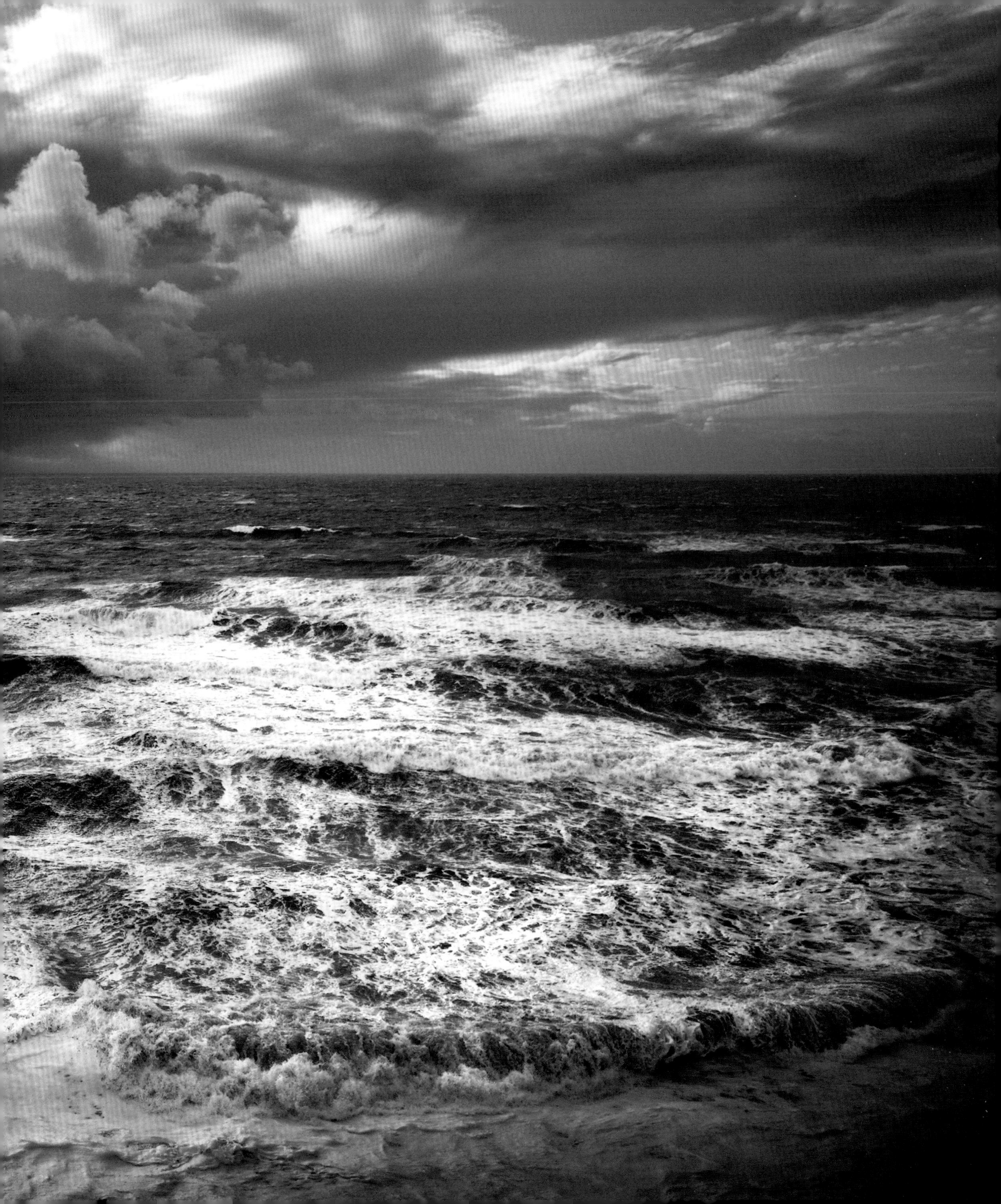

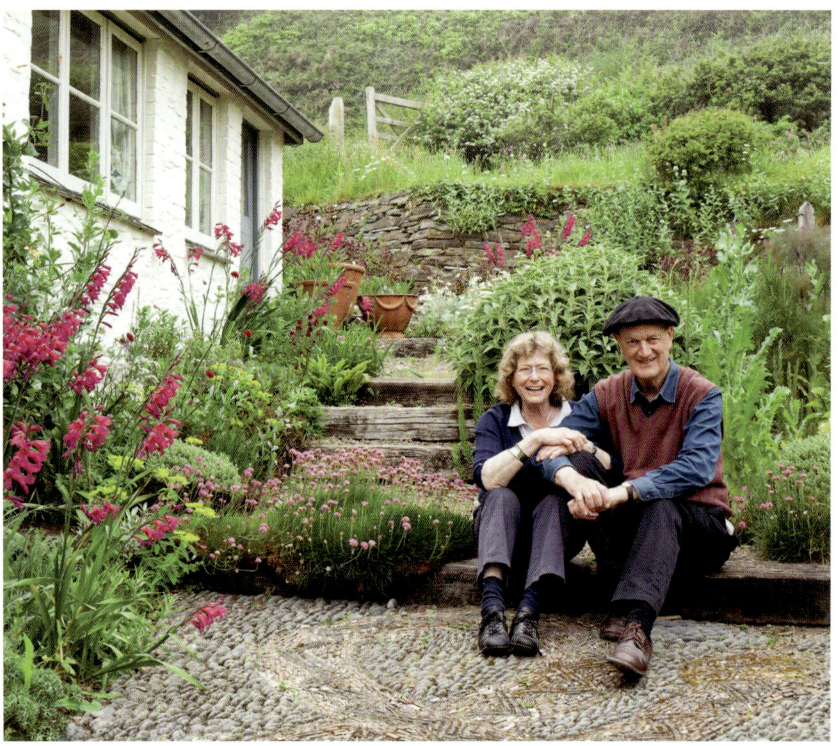

Shared Lives

Creative couples have often worked together, sometimes influenced by one another and sometimes independent. The creative relationship is unique to each pair. Some make fireworks together, others are completely complementary.

Andrew and Briony Lawson have worked alongside each other for over 45 years. Their shared creative energy flows in a subtle way. Their mutual passion for particular beautiful spaces has made a platform for the art of both of them. In their working lives they have constantly provided support and encouragement for each other, in their sculpture, paintings and drawing. And throughout their partnership, it has been the joy and stimulation of their surroundings that has provided their shared canvas.

Shared Visions Shared Lives
Briony & Andrew Lawson
at West Mill

*Published in 2017 by Impress
Editorial Department [156]
95 Wilton Road
London, SW1V 1BZ
Impress-publishing.com*

*Copyright – 2017.
All rights reserved.*

ISBN *978-0-9955540-6-1*

*Concept & Editing:
Susie Lawson*

*Photography
Andrew Lawson*

*Design by Prof. Phil Cleaver
assisted by Kay Kim
of et al design consultants*

*Printed for dlm creative
by Geoff Neal*

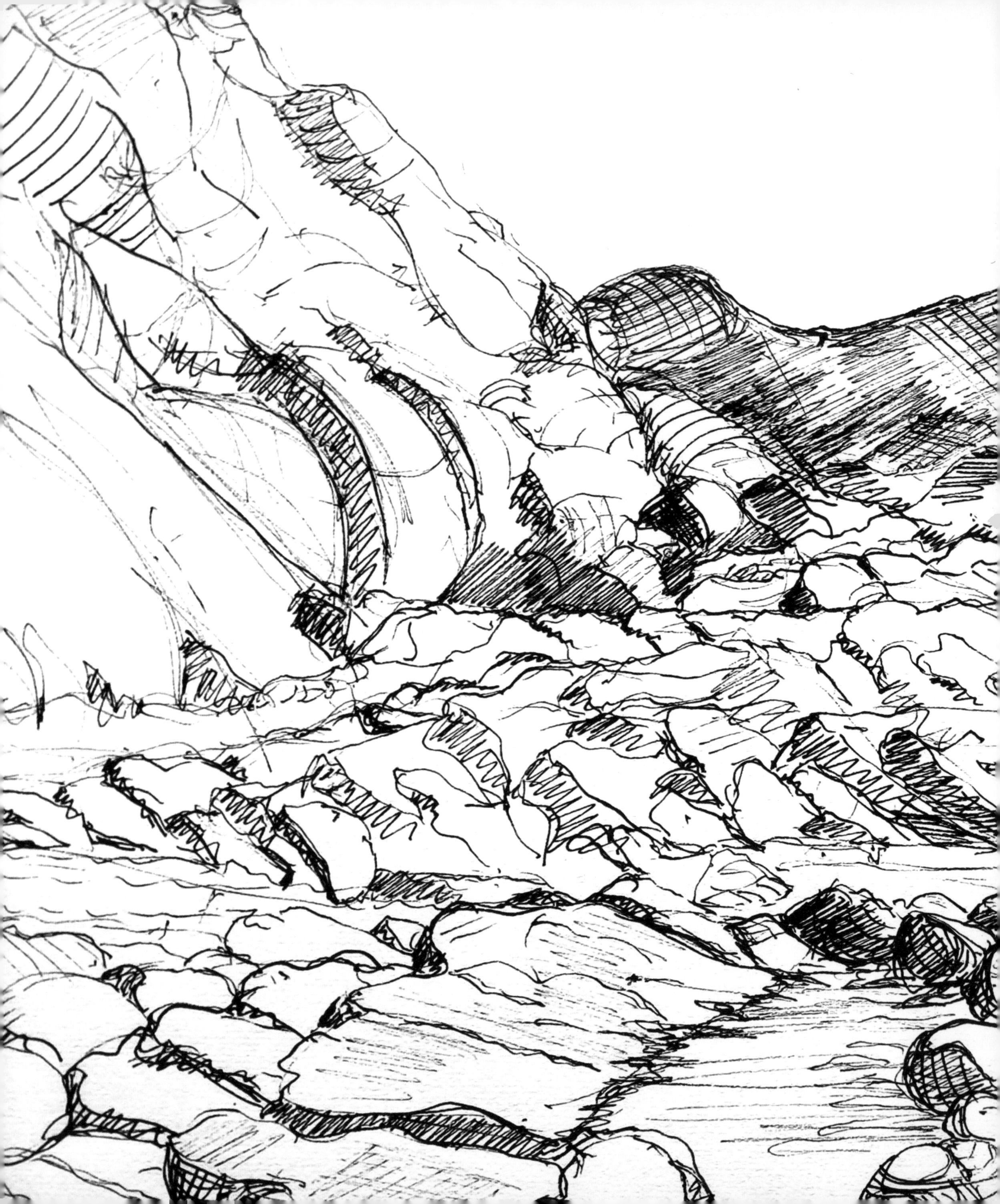